Mina Ho Ferrante

Roses
from the Crimson Rock

an illustrated memoir

Editors: Bryan Mahoney and Marcy Dewey Mahoney

Proofreaders: Nu Ho, Joseph Ferrante and Mai Lien Van Tran

Book design: Elwood Ho

Cover art: Mina Ho Ferrante

Illustrators: Dylan Loomis
            Phan Xuân Hạ
            Mina Ho Ferrante

Copyright © 2025 Mina Ho Ferrante

Published 2025. All rights reserved. Manufactured in the United States of America.

This publication is protected by Copyright, and permission should be obtained from the publisher prior to any prohibited reproduction, storage in a retrieval system, or transmission in any form or by any means, electronic, mechanical, photocopying, recording, or likewise. To obtain permission(s) to use material from this work, please submit a written request to minaho2010@yahoo.com

ISBN: 9798282074239

Printed in the United States of America

This book honors my ancestors

and is a tribute to my parents and family.

To my beloved father, late mother, siblings, aunts, uncles, and every relative who have stood by me through all hardship. Thank you for your unwavering strength, love, support, and protection; without each of you, I would not be here.

A heartfelt thanks to the family members who shared countless hours of our interviews; without these conversations, this book would not exist.

Some of the names of the Vietnamese individuals in this book have been changed to preserve their anonymity while living in Vietnam.

This book also features a variety of illustration styles because I wanted to finish it quickly for my dad to read. I enlisted help from family members to speed up the process, adding to the charm of our family project, with each person bringing their unique talents to life.

FAMILY TREE

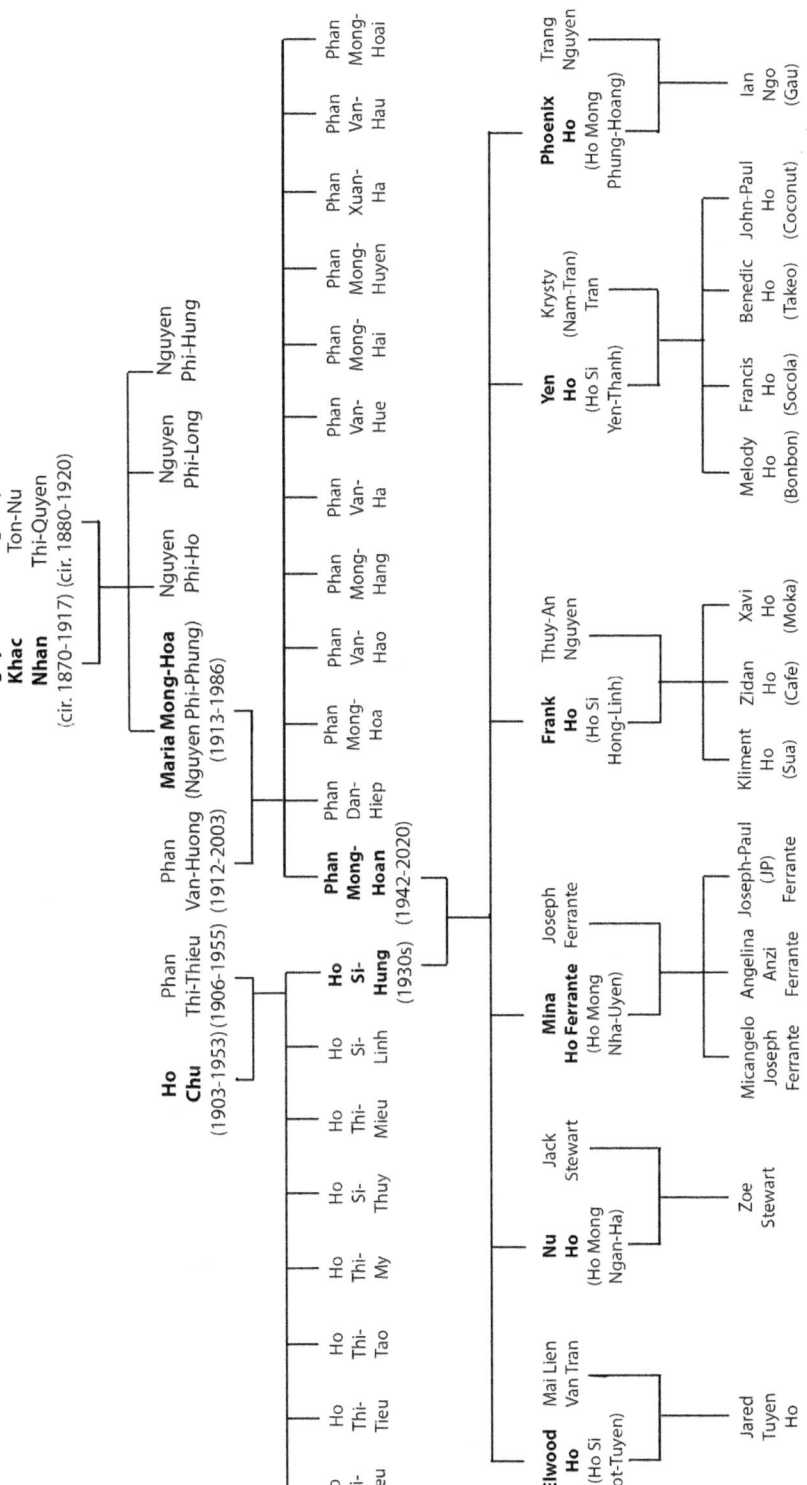

Introduction

In 2014, I began writing this book to record my family's history—from my ancestors' roles as artists and teachers in Vietnam, to my parents' escape from the communists and journey to California, to my children, who grew up without knowing the hardships my siblings and I endured. Balancing the care of my three young children, rebuilding my career after a decade as a stay-at-home mom, and staying active in my community left little time for writing.

Yet, with unwavering support from my loved ones, I kept going. Along the way, I faced challenges and setbacks, including a global pandemic, the loss of my mother, complex personal relationships, and the ongoing responsibility of caring for three teenagers. Still, I stayed committed to this work.

This book is a heartfelt gift to our remarkable parents, who devoted their lives to ensuring our safety and happiness. We lost Mom during the difficult COVID years. Now, as Dad reaches an age where each day feels like a precious blessing, I resolve to finish this book quickly.

I want him to hold this tribute—a book that honors both Mom and Dad, who have been our beacons of hope, strength, and guidance, especially in life's darkest moments.

It also honors the incredible individuals who shaped my life. Our aunts and uncles helped raise my siblings and me, protecting us from the dangers of war. My grandmother was a constant source of wisdom, sharing valuable teachings on spirituality and compassion. Our cousins and extended family brought us joy, comfort, and unconditional love, while friends brightened the most challenging days with their kindness.

In 2017, I returned to Vietnam, retracing my father's journey and connecting with the difficult past he endured. I found myself in the very places where he and his siblings grew up, where my grandparents tragically lost their lives, and where his family struggled to survive and thrive.

Beside my ancestors' graves, in a gentle mist with flashes of lightning, my uncle Lĩnh lit incense and offered prayers. In that solemn moment, he asked our ancestors to grant me wisdom and strength to honor our family's legacy. Since then, I have felt their presence daily, like guardian angels guiding me. I am determined to see this mission through, and I feel as though I possess a superpower.

This book features various illustration styles because I wanted to finish it quickly for my dad. I enlisted help from family members to speed up the process, adding to the charm of our family project, with each person bringing their unique talents to life.

With deep gratitude and love, I offer this book as a tribute to the resilience, love, and unfaltering bonds that have shaped my family. May its pages resonate with the spirit of our beloved parents, honoring our departed mother's legacy and celebrating our revered father. Let it also capture the essence of our cherished ancestors and the collective strength of our family, relatives, and friends.

Mina Ho Ferrante
also as known as Hồ Mộng Nhã Uyển

Contents

Prologue — 1

Chapter 1: The Land Reform — 6

Chapter 2: Crossing the Border to Laos — 30

Chapter 3: Mom's Family — 42

Chapter 4: War — 81

Chapter 5: Living in Exile — 129

Chapter 6: Dad's Siblings — 167

Chapter 7: The Escape Plan — 189

Chapter 8: The Journey to a New Land — 205

Chapter 9: Staying Behind — 226

Chapter 10: Nomadic Life — 235

Chapter 11: Together at Last — 270

Epilogue — 293

Prologue

Vietnam is a breathtaking country, although it has experienced numerous wars.

For more than a thousand years, it persistently fought against Chinese domination. Then it endured more than 60 years of French colonization, followed by a protracted civil war lasting over 20 years.

The ravages of war, violence, and enduring poverty have fatigued the country.

However, amidst these hardships is the unwavering kindness and compassion of the Vietnamese people. They remain hopeful and resilient. Each Vietnamese person has a story to share—a narrative of unyielding roots that continue to flourish like magnificent flowers despite their challenging surroundings.

It's a story of roses that thrive from crimson rocks.

That's my family's story.

I grew up in Vietnam during a time of war.

In the spring of 1975, I was only six years old. I lived with my family in Đà Nẵng.

I vividly recall seeing people streaming into the city from the northern regions. News spread that the North Vietnamese forces were advancing southward, and in response, panic set in. People began to flee.

My father, the principal of Đà Nẵng Tech School, made the compassionate decision to open its gates and transform the schoolyard into a haven for refugees.

Every day, my siblings and I would watch American military helicopters hover above the schoolyard, dropping bags of much needed sustenance for the displaced individuals. It was a remarkable sight.

Let me tell you his story.
And someday, I want you to tell the story to others.

Chapter 1: The Land Reform

(This chapter is written from Dad's perspective.
The information comes from recordings of his conversations,
his memoir, and countless times
he shared stories with family and friends.)

Life in Nghệ An

I came from a beautiful, peaceful town where most people were farmers. The name of the town is Nghệ An, and it is located in North Vietnam.

My father, his father, the father of his father, and so many generations before that worked very hard. Through their hard work, they acquired vast amounts of land.

They were known for their kindness. During famines, they opened their food stores to help those in need in our village.

During that time, there had been rumors that the communist government was planning to confiscate wealth from the landowners. Trying to stay peaceful with the authorities, my father faithfully made regular contributions to the North Vietnam government.

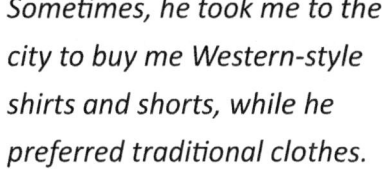

I have fond memories of my father.

Sometimes, he took me to the city to buy me Western-style shirts and shorts, while he preferred traditional clothes.

He also bought me a bicycle from the French-occupied province, which was considered a luxury item at the time.

My father occasionally took me on hunting trips. It was more of a sport for us. We both would ride on one large horse up to a high mountain, where we'd rendezvous with a hunter in a small hut. Although the plan was to hunt late at night, my father and I often ended up sleeping in the hut, skipping the entire event while the hunter went out to search for deer. On one occasion, he caught a pregnant deer. My father felt uneasy about it, and we never went hunting again.

I also have beautiful memories of my mom. She was a hardworking woman who took care of everything in our household. She instructed helpers who came to mill the rice after the harvest.

Once a year, she organized the Ancestor Memorial Feast to which all our relatives and neighbors in the village were invited. There was plenty of food, and I enjoyed playing with my many cousins.

When all the work was finished, at the end of the day, my mother and older sisters would bathe at a pond near our house. I would wade in the water, listening to their conversations and laughter. It made me feel happy and peaceful.

From a very young age, my parents and everyone in our extended family ensured I understood the importance of my role. As the clan heir, it was my duty to study diligently and strive for excellence to one day bring honor to our ancestors and our family name. Failure was not an option.

Since my village school only offered classes up to the fifth grade, my family sent me to a nearby city to continue my education. I could only return home during school breaks or in the summer.

The political change

Since the early 1950s, I had witnessed propaganda programs promoting Land Reform and the unsettling events that unfolded during the Land Distribution campaign in China, which resulted in the deaths of approximately one million landlords, along with the confiscation of their property.

During this campaign, the Chinese Communist Party incited the anger and resentment of impoverished peasants towards landlords, subjecting them to verbal and physical abuse and ultimately executing them. They aimed to eradicate all social classes except for the working class.

The same thing was about to happen in Vietnam.

In 1953, during my ninth-grade year, I witnessed a march led by farmers organized by the Labor Party. They proudly carried banners praising the "Land Reform" movement. The mob looked angry and dangerous. It made me feel nervous.

At that time, my classmates and I were forced to attend The People's Court, a frightening gathering where landowners were brought before the crowd one by one. Disturbingly, these innocent individuals were accused of crimes they hadn't committed. The mob roared with delight while their families trembled in terror.

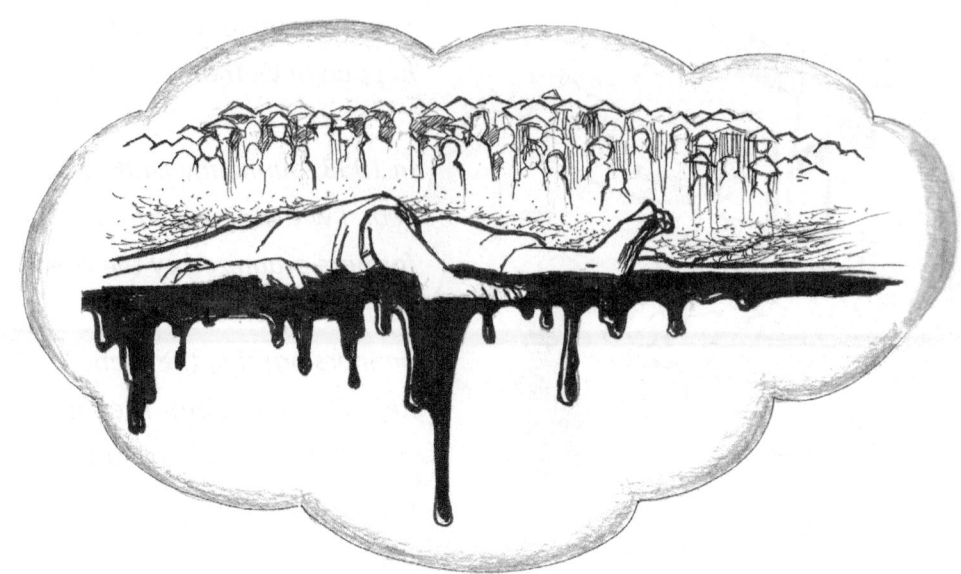

Shockingly, the trial concluded with the execution of the landowners in front of the horrified crowd and their anguished families.

These acts of terror deeply frightened me. I couldn't help but worry about my father's safety since he was also a landowner. The fear for his well-being consumed my thoughts. I longed to return home but I was forbidden to leave until the school year ended.

Tragedy at home

When I was allowed to leave school, I borrowed a bicycle to travel home. Upon reaching my village, I was immediately halted by public security men on the outskirts. They swiftly escorted me to a confined room and held me there.

They interrogated me for three days. Throughout the ordeal, I remained composed, refusing to show emotions, especially anger. Eventually, they deemed me "safe for the people" and released me.

The nightmare unfolded before me. Upon arriving home, I discovered that everything had been taken from my family by the authorities. My father had been executed because he was a landowner. My grandmother, mother, and younger siblings were forced to relocate to an old dilapidated shack at the edge of the village.

My mother clung to me, weeping as she shared the news of my father's murder. My grandmother spent her days lying on the floor, incessantly calling out my father's name. My younger siblings were hungry and sorrowful. Mỹ was 11, Thụy was 8, Miều was 5, and Lĩnh was barely two years old.

We endured a year in that hut. My mother, my siblings, and I worked tirelessly in the small, rocky yard, growing vegetables and potatoes. Our meager harvest barely kept us alive. We were always hungry, and I remember my mother eating very little so we could have more.

Malnutrition took a toll on my mother's health. She suffered constant pain when she walked since her feet were swollen. Nevertheless, she never ceased working.

As the year ended, in keeping with cultural custom, people would go to the cemetery to tend to their loved ones' graves; during this time, we were allowed to visit my father's burial place. While we were there, my mother showed me the high mound of earth where my father had been executed.

At the base of the mound, bloodstains remained as evidence. I reached out and touched the stains, collapsing to the ground. I wanted to scream, but I remained silent. I wanted to cry, but no tears came.

When they murdered my father and other landowners, they not only took lives but also shattered our peaceful culture and destroyed the harmony of our people. The supposed Land Reform for wealth distribution was a deceitful lie, a means for the Communist Party to seize people's property violently.

Trial again

One day, we heard rumors of another round of trials targeting landowners. I was 18, and my mother feared I might be next for execution. One night, she handed me a small bundle of potatoes and rice wrapped in cloth and begged me to flee the village.

Please stay alive so that someday you will come back to help your family.

My mother watched me until I was out of sight. I glanced back. She was frail and vulnerable in the darkness. It was the last time I saw her. Each step I took away from her weighed heavily on my heart.

I walked throughout the night and day until I felt I had distanced myself enough from my village. Then, I hitched a ride on a cow-drawn wagon headed toward Hanoi.

Hanoi was a bustling city where I found refuge and worked as a tutor for familiar families. I also secretly managed to send money to support my mother and siblings.

Not long after I left the village, I received the distressing news that my family was again subjected to trial. This time, they were evicted from the small yard where we had painstakingly cultivated our food. My mother, grandmother, and young siblings were forced to relocate to a crumbling straw hut without any land. The children suffered from hunger, my grandmother's health deteriorated rapidly, and my mother's illness worsened.

One day, despite her swollen feet, my mother walked to her sister's home a few villages away. At the time, the government prohibited contact with the landowners since they were condemned as "the enemies of the People." Her sister quickly gave her a potato, which mother hid in her hair bun. Her feet were hurting, causing her to walk slowly and unsteadily. As she entered her village, where her starving children were waiting for her, she was stopped and searched by the guards, who discovered the potato. They publicly shamed her for "stealing from the People" in front of the village.

My mother knew that no one dared to assist our family due to the pervasive fear of the government. Perhaps that's why she chose to end her own life by jumping into the village well one night. She must have hoped that, in her absence, people would extend their help to the children.

Following my mother's tragic death, my grandmother succumbed to starvation. My young siblings were left to beg for food on the streets, desperate to survive.

Eventually, farmers from distant villages came. Each took in one of my siblings as house chores or field labor helpers.

(Readers will find more details about this separation later in Chapter 6)

Upon learning about my mother's heartbreaking death, I secretly returned to the village, determined to find my siblings. I walked from one village to another, diligently searching for them. Finally, I located each of them, living separately in different homes, far apart.

My siblings faced arduous lives, laboring to help their adoptive families with household chores and agricultural tasks. They lived in poverty, but it was the only way they could survive the tragic circumstances that had befallen our family. Though filled with immense sorrow, I bid them farewell, promising we would reunite someday.

With a heavy heart, I began to plan my escape to South Vietnam.

(End of Dad's narration)

Chapter 2: Crossing the Border to Laos

In 1954, the Geneva Conference divided my country into North and South Vietnam. At the conference, Vietnamese civilians were given the choice to move freely to either North or South Vietnam between 1954 and 1956.

However, the government in Dad's village purposely didn't inform the public about this relocation program, so Dad and his family were unaware of it and remained where they were.

In 1955, Dad and his cousin Khâm sought asylum at the French consulate in Hà Nội. The staff at the French Embassy let them hide in the attic for one day but eventually turned them away, returning them to the North Vietnamese authorities.

They were then imprisoned in Hoả Lò prison for 18 months. Known in America as "The Hanoi Hilton," this prison was notorious for its harsh and miserable conditions, including insufficient food, an extremely unsanitary environment, and cruel treatment from the prison staff.

At first, Dad was kept in a room tightly packed with other prisoners. There was hardly any air to breathe, and the stench of unwashed bodies was putrid. The prisoners were covered with mange and scabs, the results of malnutrition and unsanitary conditions. To avoid the crowded room, Dad chose to sit near the area where prisoners defecated and urinated; since the smell was nauseating, fewer people were in that area. In the mornings, the guards selected Dad and a few other young prisoners who were still strong enough to carry the barrels of feces to the dump. Though the task was filthy, Dad was glad to get out for some air.

Eventually, Dad was moved into an isolated cell. It was a small, dark, stone room that was always damp and cold. The only view outside was through a small hole in the wall. This dark cell was infested with rats and cockroaches, and he was often left hungry. Dad couldn't decide which was worse: the stinky, cramped room or being alone in this dark hell.

The following year, the Hungarian Uprising, a 12-day countrywide rebellion against Hungary's communist government, occurred. To avoid a similar incident in Vietnam, the communist government tried to ease its strict rules. As a result, it released low-profile political prisoners, including my dad and his cousin.

After his release in 1957, Dad found solace in befriending Catholic priests in Hà Nội, who reached out to assist troubled young students. However, the authorities disapproved of this, so in 1958, they sent him back to Thanh Hoá, near his hometown of Nghệ An.

While under house arrest in Thanh Hoá, Dad needed to find a way to support himself. The authorities assigned "agents" to watch him; these "agents" were villagers who were as poor and hungry as Dad was. They often went up the mountains to search for tiger bones and then sold the bones to a medicine man in the village who brewed them to make medicine for back pain and arthritis. They allowed Dad to accompany them, earning a little for his daily food.

Eventually, Dad secretly formed an acquaintance with two young men who knew how to cross the border into Laos through the mountainous jungle terrain. These men were often hired as guides by individuals seeking tiger bones. Despite her own  poverty, Dad's eldest sister, Thiệu, managed to provide him with two silver cups to pay the men to help him escape to Laos. Those two silver cups were among the very few valuables she possessed.

One night, the two guides took Dad, his cousin Khâm, and their friend Duẩn to a hut in a field. They were told to sleep there and start the escape early the following day. For dinner, they cooked rice inside bamboo sticks. Dad couldn't sleep that night because he worried about being caught, but the two guides seemed relaxed, to his astonishment, as if it were just a picnic trip.

The trails up the steep and rugged mountain were challenging. On the first day, they ventured deep into the jungle without seeing anyone. In the morning, they continued their ascent deeper into the jungle and encountered a group of Laotians descending toward Vietnamese villages, carrying baskets filled with opium to trade.

They came across a young man cheerfully playing his flute while walking. When asked where he was heading, he said that he often crossed the jungle to visit his girlfriend in the next village. My father was impressed by his determination.

They followed him to a small village, where Dad saw pictures of the Laotian king hanging on the walls of the huts. This assured him they were in Laotian territory and safe from the Vietnamese communists.

The two guides bid farewell to Dad, Khâm, and Duẩn as they needed to return home. Dad and his group continued their journey deeper into Laos.

During this journey, Dad was amazed by the hospitality of the Laotian people.

They were invited into Laotian homes and were offered sticky rice and boiled corn freshly picked from the fields. Many Laotians made their own guns and opium. They provided the group with opium to smoke from bamboo pipes. Dad didn't smoke but enjoyed the corn and delicious sticky rice.

A Laotian man offered them a ride on his small boat to the nearest Laos government station the next day. As they traveled down the river that flowed rapidly through the jungle, monkeys in the trees screamed loudly at them. The water ran fast and rough, so Dad realized it must have been challenging for the man to paddle against the stream on his return journey.

Finally, they arrived at a Laos border station, where they were allowed to stay. They were given lodging and were well fed with sticky rice and bamboo soup. Dad was excited to find beef in the soup and thought it was fantastic.

During the day, Dad explored and stumbled upon a small church with a library, but no one was inside. Walking around, he met a Vietnamese nun who offered him some wine.

A few days later, the people at the border station put Dad and his group on a bus to Vientiane, Laos' capital. There, they were transferred to the central police station and given a private room. Dad explored again and found the South Vietnam Consulate. The Ambassador kindly allowed Dad and his group to stay at the consulate.

In July 1958, the South Vietnam Ambassador in Laos arranged to fly all the refugees, like Dad and his group, to Sài Gòn, Vietnam. The following month, he met a Catholic priest named Luận. Reverend Cao Văn Luận helped Dad settle in Hue and register to study at Hue University. Rev. Luận remained Dad's sponsor and a good friend until the priest died in 1986.

With Dad fully enrolled in school, he prepared himself for the next stage of his life, which involved getting married and starting a family.

Chapter 3:
Mom's Family

In 1960, Dad met Mom in Huế.

Huế is an ancient city in Vietnam where the Nguyễn Dynasty resided in the 19th and early 20th centuries. This dreamy and poetic land is the home of beautiful royal mausoleums, temples, and shrines, which have witnessed the triumphs and tragedies of past dynasties.

They say the misty, peaceful Hương (Perfume) River and the mythical, sacred, ancient Thiên Mụ Temple have given Huế women a unique and enchanting beauty that leaves a lasting impression on those who see it.

Great-grandparents

My great-grandfather was Nguyễn Khắc Nhân (1870-1917), who worked for the Vietnamese Emperor Thành Thái, who reigned from 1889 to 1907.

Portrait of great-grandpa Nguyễn Khắc Nhân and great-grandma Công Huyền Thị Quyên - Watercolor painting by their son Nguyễn Phi Hùng, c. 1942

My great-grandfather's job was to record what was happening at the king's court by painting the events with watercolor on rice paper.

Artwork by great-grandfather Nguyễn Khắc Nhân, c. 1907

According to family records, around 1907, while serving Emperor Thành Thái in Quảng Trị, my great-grandfather met the great minister Nguyễn Hữu Bài and Father Père Léopold Michel Cadière, a French scholar and missionary. Father Cadière commissioned him to paint the La Vang Temple, and in 1913, Father Cadière printed the image in large quantities to distribute in Catholic churches.

My great-grandfather also painted many portraits of the emperor's officials.

This is a portrait of Mr. Hoàng Hữu Xứng, the Minister of Education of the Nguyen Dynasty from Emperor Tu-Duc to Emperor Thành Thái in the second half of the 19th century. This painting was done a few years before 1900, when Mr. Hoàng Hữu Xứng retired.

Hiệp biện Đại học sĩ
HOÀNG HỮU XỨNG
(1831 - 1905)
(Chân dung do Cụ Nguyễn Khắc Nhân
Họa sĩ cung đình
vẽ theo lối truyền thần ký ức)

Artwork by great-grandfather Nguyễn Khắc Nhân, c. 1900 or earlier
Image: Courtesy from the Hoang family's website
http://www.hoangtocbichkhe.com/ho-hoang/tin-tuc-hoang-toc/anh-hoang-huu-xung

About Mr. Hoàng Hữu Xứng, he wrote many valuable Vietnamese historical books. One of his most famous was Đại Nam Quốc Cương Giới Vựng Biên (Great Vietnam Boundary), in which he documented and recorded the geography of Vietnam, including all provinces from North to South.

This map of Vietnam of the time, Đại Nam Quốc Cương Giới Vựng Biên, by Mr. Hoàng Hữu Xứng is being preserved by Mr. Hoàng Phủ Ngọc Phan and his family (currently living in Thủ Đức, Vietnam) under the responsibility of the patriarch—courtesy of the Hoàng family's website.

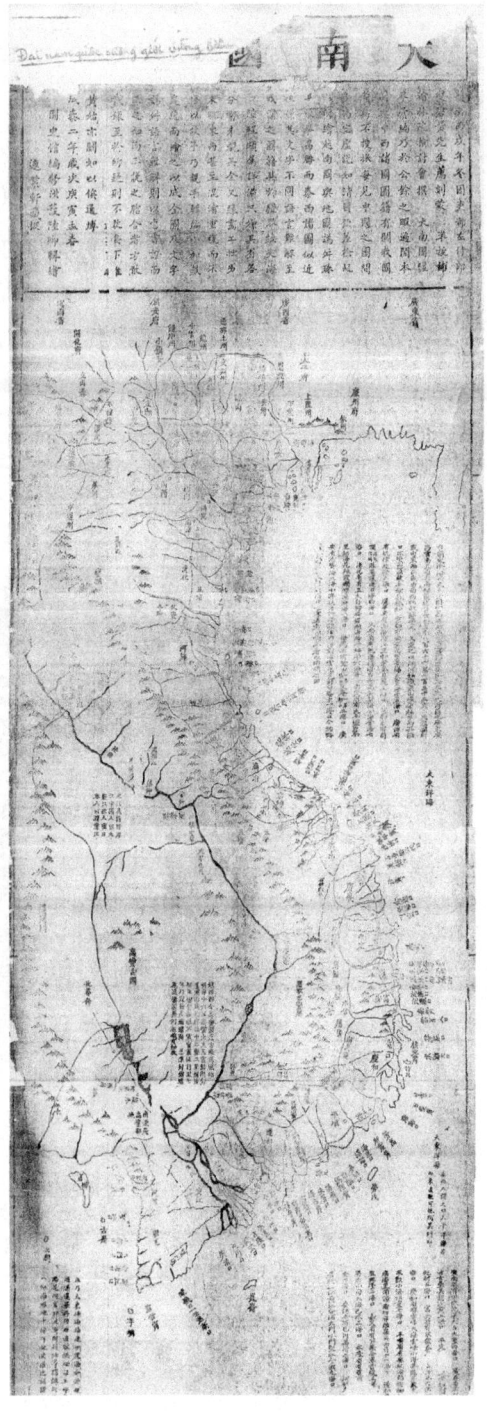

Map of the Great Vietnam Boundary, by Mr. Hoàng Hữu Xứng, 1887
Image: Courtesy from the Hoang family's website http://www.hoangtocbichkhe.com/ho-hoang/nhan-vat/hhx-tac-gia/

Grandma's siblings

My great-grandfather had three sons who were well know artists in Huế.

One of them was Nguyễn Phi Hùng, a nationally renowned artist during his time. Many of his artworks were featured in the established art journal Bulletin Des Amis Du Vieux Hue from 1934 to 1944.

A cover art by Nguyễn Phi Hùng for the magazine Bulletin Des Amis Du Vieux Hue depicting a Hue temple, c. 1939

Since there were no photo or video cameras then, his paintings and drawings help us see Vietnamese society and its culture during the early 19th century.

An Illustration of a Wedding by Nguyễn Phi Hùng, c. 1934

His artworks show how people dressed and celebrated events like weddings and what the buildings and palaces looked like.

A Royal Woman by Nguyễn Phi Hùng, c. 1942

A Gentleman in his formal outfit by Nguyễn Phi Hùng, c. 1938

A music Book Cover by Nguyễn Phi Hùng

Great-Uncle Nguyễn Phi Hùng was also famous for creating art for book covers and albums that evoke a melancholic reminiscence of Vietnam's past, particularly the pre-colonization era.

Planche III. — Nids d'Hirondelles des Culao-Cham, grandeur naturelle
(d'après une peinture de M. Phi - Hổ).

The siblings' oldest brother is Nguyễn Phi Hổ. He also illustrated for Bulletin Des Amis Du Vieux Hue. In one of his drawings, he depicted the issue of harvesting swiftlet birds' nests to sell to companies. These nests are highly valued because they are rare, and some Asians believe that consuming them can improve their health and appearance. The drawing showed that the birds were left without a place to live when people took the swiftlet nests. Even more troubling, the collectors often discarded eggs and chicks, leaving them to die on the ground.

Planche II. — Collocalia des côtes d'Annam, grandeur naturelle
(sur une Aquarelle de M. Phi - Hổ).

A Swiftlet Bird and the Broken Nest by Nguyễn Phi Hổ, c. 1930, from the Bulletin Des Amis Du Vieux Hue

Grandma's second older brother was Great-Uncle Nguyễn Phi Long. He was also an artist and participated in art events with his siblings. More about this will follow later in this chapter.

An artwork by Nguyễn Phi Long.
Image: Courtesy from Reverend Anton Nguyễn Trường Thăng's blog
https://antontruongthang.wordpress.com/wp-content/uploads/2011/02/img_6884.jpg

Grandma's special story

The youngest daughter of my great-grandfather was Maria Mộng Hoa; her birth certificate name was Nguyễn Phi Phụng (1913-1986). She was my grandmother.

When I was younger, I often heard the legend of how Grandma came to be. This story was published in Catholic magazines before 1975 and is now available on the Catholic Pilgrimage Network website.

Self-portrait by Maria Mộng-Hoa, pastel on paper, c. 1976

One day, Great-Grandfather visited the sacred Our Lady of La Vang shrine. This special place was dedicated to honoring Mother Mary, who appeared there in 1789. The Lady of La Vang was believed to be able to answer prayers and provide comfort and guidance.

At the shrine, Great Grandfather prayed, "Dear Lady of La Vang, please bless us with a daughter. She will belong to you, and everything she does in her life will be to glorify your name."

When he returned home, his wife eagerly shared her remarkable dream. In her dream, she saw a breathtaking woman dressed in a pristine white and blue gown. The lady held splendid flower wreaths in her hands and gently offered one of these exquisite wreaths to my great-grandmother. Overwhelmed with awe, Great-Grandmother asked for more, but the lady just smiled and disappeared, leaving behind a sense of wonder.

Nine months later, Grandma was born on August 15, 1913, the day of the Assumption of the Blessed Virgin Mary. They named her Maria Dream of Flower to honor the Lady of Lavang, fulfilling the great-grandfather's prayer at the sacred shrine.

Each time I hear that story, it reminds me that Grandma was very special, a blessed gift from heaven. Though she is no longer with us, I pray to her in difficult times; it's comforting to know that there's someone to turn to spiritually and find solace in times of need.

My great-grandfather passed away in 1917 when Grandma was only four years old. Fortunately, she had three older brothers who helped raise her and taught her all they knew about art.

Under their training, Grandma became very skilled at drawing and painting. She also learned about art by reading art history books and magazines imported from France. Ever since she was little, it was evident that Grandma possessed a natural talent for art, as if it flowed effortlessly through her veins.

Grandma first gained recognition at just 18 years old, when she was awarded a Gold Medal at the Huế Fine Arts Exhibition in 1931.

On September 25, 1932, a grand painting exhibition was held at the French Embassy of Central Vietnam in the imperial capital of Huế. The event was attended by Emperor Bảo Đại, alongside French and Vietnamese officials, notable figures from Huế, and guests from various provinces. The exhibition featured artists from both France and Vietnam's Đông Dương (Indochina), including Grandma Mộng Hoa and her brothers, Phi Long and Phi Hùng. Grandma was 19 at the time.

Praying- *1935 - Pastel on paper*
(Auction on MutralArt.com)

Praying, by Maria Mộng-Hoa, pastel on paper, c. 1935

In 1936, she took part in another major exhibition, this time organized by France at the Royal Court of Huế. Grandma often spoke fondly of this special occasion—one of her favorite memories—when the legendary Charlie Chaplin visited the exhibition and personally shook her hand.

Grandma and her family

Grandma became well-known and popular in Huế for her talent, kindness, and elegant beauty.

Friends and relatives often came to her with their troubles. She would listen, offer advice if needed, and help them financially if they required assistance. People loved her and spoke highly of her.

Grandma, 1950

Grandma painted portraits and landscapes and sold her art to support her large family of twelve, which included ten beautiful and intelligent children. She was the first female artist in Huế to have her own gallery. Her favorite subjects to paint were portraits of her husband, her lovely children, and religious themes.

*Tuổi Mộng Mơ (Dream-Filled Days)
Pastel on paper by
Maria Mộng Hoa, c. 1964s*

This pastel portrait of my mom by Grandma was auctioned in Sài Gòn, Vietnam, and acquired by Mr. Luân Khánh, an entrepreneur and antique collector. Miraculously, this painting (c. 1964) remained intact throughout the war and years of being lost. It seemed to have traveled a long journey over the past 49 years.

After the Vietnam War ended in 1975, this artwork came into the possession of an art collector who lived on Trần Huy Liệu Street, District 3, Sài Gòn. It was then acquired by the late Rev. Nguyễn Hữu Triết, whose extensive collection included rare Vietnamese artworks from the early 20th century and the most extensive collection of antique lamps in Vietnam.

In 2011, this artwork was transferred to the late Rev. Anton Nguyễn Tường Thăng, a researcher passionate about the history and art of Hue before 1975. He had been writing articles about my grandma's family, from her royal artist father to her siblings and descendants.

After Rev. Anton Nguyễn Tường Thăng passed away, his close disciple, Thái Lão Tà, auctioned the painting, hoping a great art collector would acquire and preserve it. That was how the painting came into Mr. Luân Khánh's possession.

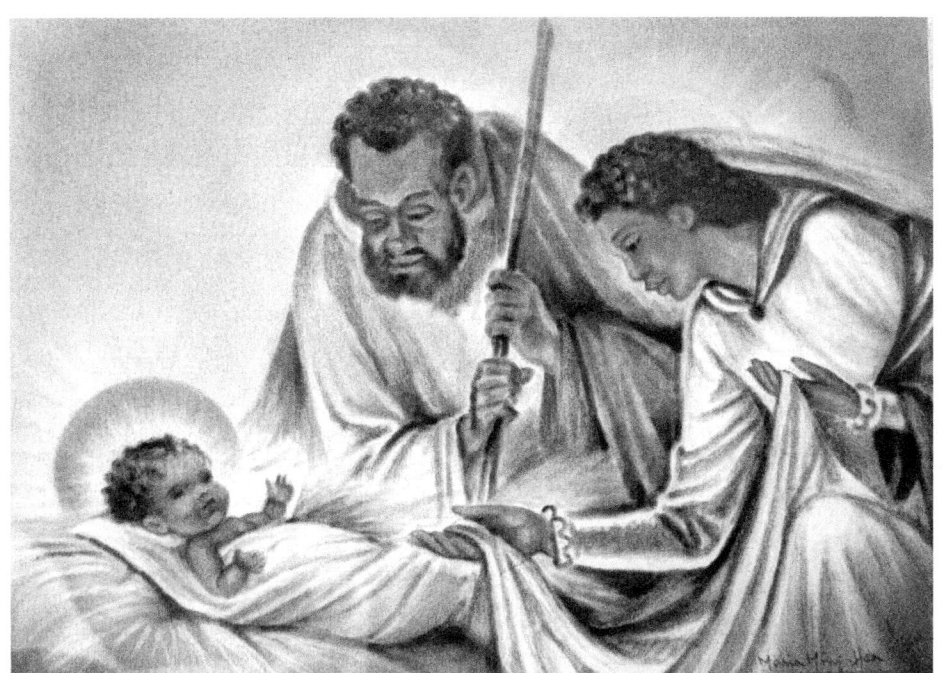

The Nativity - Pastel on paper by Maria Mộng Hoa, 1970

This pastel artwork (c. 1970) was commissioned by Mr. Ernest Thompson. At the time, Mr. Thompson was 21 years old and drafted to fight in Vietnam against the North Vietnamese.

When his troop was posted in Đà Nẵng for a week, he spent his free time wandering the city and stumbled upon my grandma's art gallery. Amid the horrors of war, he found sanctuary in my grandma's little art room, where paintings filled the walls. Despite the language barrier, they shared stories and laughter.

In April 2024, Mr. Thompson returned to Vietnam for a visit. Passing through Đà Nẵng, he searched for my grandma. When he couldn't find her, he enlisted his tour guide, Ms. Jolie Nguyen, for help. Ms. Jolie's research revealed that my grandma had passed away, but she found my contact information via Facebook. Words

*Portrait of a Vietnamese Woman
Pastel on paper by
Maria Mộng Hoa, c. 1930s*

cannot describe how excited Mr. Thompson was when he called me. He shared that he still remembers the laughter they shared 54 years ago.

During that week in Đà Nẵng in 1970, he visited the gallery daily. He commissioned my grandma to create a Nativity scene with a special request. As an African American, Mr. Thompson was frustrated that all Nativity scenes he saw were portrayed with Caucasian features. He wanted my grandma to create a Nativity scene he could relate to. Mr. Thompson left Vietnam with this painting, which has accompanied him everywhere. Thanks to Mr. Thompson's care, the artwork is still in excellent condition today.

In the 1950s, Grandma and Grandpa pioneered new technologies and gadgets and were "avant-garde" business adventurers. They bought the newly introduced cameras, opened a photo studio, and opened a record store equipped with shiny record players when these were still a rarity in Vietnam.

Grandma and Grandpa once turned part of their duplex into an inn. It quickly became a popular meeting place for local elites and intellectuals to discuss art, music, literature, and other social topics.

People loved Grandma's warm hospitality, and the inn provided a good income for the family. However, there were concerns about my mom and her sisters, who were beautiful and soon reaching marriageable age. Many people advised Grandma to close the inn to protect these young women's reputation. Living in a very conservative society, Grandma had no choice but to listen to the people and close the inn.

In addition to painting, Grandma also taught drawing and painting at the Huế College of Art. Her students loved her.

Life was peaceful until, in the Spring of 1968, which was historically called the "Tết Offensive," the North Vietnamese army attacked Huế and killed thousands of people living in the city—many of whom were buried alive by the North Vietnamese army in mass graves.

Witnessing thousands of people wailing with grief and pain by the endless lines of coffins waiting to be buried was heartbreaking. Grandma moved from Huế to Đà Nẵng and lived with her children.

In Đà Nẵng, Grandma opened a studio, and her art gallery became well known.

Grandma and Grandpa's children were all artistic and creative in their own ways. Some of them chose to follow Grandma's art journey.

Uncle Hiệp

Grandpa and Grandma's eldest son was Uncle Phan Dân Hiệp. He was intelligent, charming, and had a talent for the arts. He was skilled in both English and French, loved reading, and filled his journals with poems and writings about his dreams. He also played the guitar and sang.

Because he was a former South Vietnam military officer, he was sent to a re-education camp by the communist government after the Vietnam War ended in 1975. The harsh living conditions, forced labor, and limited food almost cost him his life. The authorities released him when they saw his health fatally deteriorating.

During this tumultuous post-war time, our family had to hide in an area without access to schools. Uncle Hiệp stayed with us and tutored us for years. He taught us Vietnamese, world literature, poetry, and English. Despite his poor health from the re-education camp, he remained optimistic. He encouraged us not to worry about the uncertain future but to cherish the present, where we had a roof over our heads and loved ones around us.

Uncle Hiệp passed away in 1985 at the age of 48. He left behind his wife, Trần Thị Hoa, two daughters, Hoài Hương and Hoài Phương, three sons, Dân Việt, Dân Nam, and Quốc Cường.

When I asked my cousin Hoài Phương about her most cherished memory of her father, she described him as sweet and gentle. After he returned from the re-education camp, despite their family's poverty, he would take his five young children out together for simple walks around the city. He often played the guitar and sang to them at night, always smiling, no matter how hungry they were. That memory will stay with her forever.

Aunt Mộng Hoà

Aunt Mộng Hoà attended the Huế College of Art and, after graduating, taught at the College of Education in Qui-Nhơn. She then married uncle Trương Minh Tâm and moved to Nha-Trang, Vietnam. She dedicated her life to caring for her family, her children, and, in later years, many grandchildren.

In her rare free time, she took on painting commissions. Her artworks are elegant and hauntingly beautiful; the women in her paintings are graceful, with ebony black hair and pale, translucent skin.

Watercolor on silk by Phan Mộng Hoà, c. 1979

Aunt Hoà used to say she would paint more in the future when she had more free time. Sadly, in 2004, when she was 65 years old, she had a stroke that paralyzed half of her body. Despite this, she would sometimes try to paint using her left hand.

Until her passing in 2023, Aunt Hoà remained a cheerful presence, always making a heartfelt effort to bring joy to those around her. She was the proud mother of seven children: Trương Minh Mộng-Tuyền, Trương Minh Anh-Tuấn, Trương Minh Cát-Tín, Trương Minh Hiếu-Toàn, Trương Minh Nhật-Tân, Trương Minh Nhất-Tiến, and Trương Minh Nhã-Tiên. Along with her children, she welcomed seven sons- and daughters-in-law, 18 grandchildren, and two great-grandchildren into her growing family. One of her sons, Trương Minh Nhật-Tân, sadly passed away before her.

Even after her passing, Aunt Hoà's warmth and joyful spirit continues to live on in the hearts of her large and loving family. The next in line of the siblings was my mother, Mộng Hoàn, but more on her later.

Aunt Mộng Hằng

Mom's next sibling was five years younger than her. Aunt Mộng Hằng was always creative and resourceful in finding ways to support herself, especially during the post-war era, when many people in Vietnam struggled to make ends meet. She had remarkable beauty and a free-spirited nature, but she was not fond of conforming to rules. Although I didn't get to know Aunt Hằng well, I remember her bright personality and hearty laugh. Her laughter was so joyful and infectious that it made you want to laugh with her.

Aunt Hằng died in 2023 and was survived by her four children – Hoàng-Vũ, Tri-Túc, Hoàng-Nhân, and Tri-Tâm – and many grandchildren.

Uncle Huệ

Uncle Huệ has a romantic soul and an excellent talent for music. He was sent to a Huế Catholic Seminary by the Congregatio Sanctissimi Redemptoris (Dòng Chuá Cứu Thế) to become a priest. However, he always fell ill whenever he was at the seminary, so they sent him back home. He jokingly said that maybe he didn't have the calling to be a priest. After finishing high school at Phan Châu Trinh and graduating from Huế University of Education, he taught French at Trần Quý Cáp High School in Hội An for a year before our family had to run to our hideout from the new government in 1975.

In the late 1970s, Uncle Huệ fell in love with an alluring, pretty woman. They wrote numerous love letters during their long-distance relationship, and he created over a dozen beautiful

romantic songs dedicated to her. Fifty-five years later, despite their relationship's many ups and downs and no longer being together, Uncle Huệ still talks about her with love and tender memories.

Aunt Mộng Hài

Mộng-Hài, by Maria Mộng-Hoa pastel on paper, c. 1980

Aunt Mộng Hài's beauty was as pure as her heart. She was close to Grandma and devoted to her throughout her life. She was always by Grandma's side, caring for her every need. Aunt Hài made sure everything Grandma required was right at her fingertips. She also helped manage Grandma's finances. I can't imagine Grandma without Aunt Hài. My memory of her is that she was loving, kind, gentle, and had an easy laugh.

Aunt Mộng Huyền

Aunt Mộng Huyền was a popular teenager—very smart and incredibly beautiful. Her skin was rosy, and her black hair was shiny and soft. Her deep brown eyes were radiant and captivating, framed by thick lashes, and she had a bright, cheerful smile. She was great with people and had many friends who genuinely liked her. Young men would often drop by Grandma's art studio just for a chance to talk to my attractive aunt. To us children, Aunt Huyền was a wonderful storyteller, sharing endless tales from books or movies she had seen. She was also good at keeping us in line and taught us how to behave properly.

Uncle Bê Em

Uncle, Bê Em, one of the illustrators of this memoir, is an incredible artist. Before 1975, he attended the Huế College of Art. After 1975, when our family faced financial difficulties, he found a way to make a living by decorating interiors and painting advertising billboards for restaurants, coffee shops, and churches. When I was little, I watched him paint murals for hours and dreamed I could someday paint like him.

Uncle Út Hậu

In my grandma's family, Uncle Út Hậu is a legendary figure to us, his nieces and nephews. He was known for being rebellious. He enjoyed breaking the rules and yet could be very charming when he wanted to be. Uncle Út Hậu faced tough times in his life with substances, but as he got older, he showed incredible strength and determination in overcoming his past struggles. With the support of his family, he embraced a much healthier lifestyle, sober and substance-free. His experiences taught him valuable life lessons and inspired others facing similar challenges. In the end, Uncle Út Hậu became a strong and caring person. He peacefully passed away in May 2024, surrounded by his loving family.

Aunt Mộng Hoài (Dì Út)

Aunt Mộng Hoài was Mom's youngest sister. We endearingly called her Dì Út, meaning "the youngest aunt." Before the war ended in 1975, Dì Út lived with my family in Đà Nẵng. I remember her being a dreamy teenager, looking like a hippie, and always wearing a tight T-shirt and bell-bottom jeans. Her shoulder-length hair was soft and flowed effortlessly, framing her youthful face, which always glowed with a smile. Back then, many of Mom and Dad's students would frequently visit our house to take a quick glimpse of her.

Aunt Hoài took cooking classes at the Đà Nẵng Tech School, where Dad was the principal. She often practiced what she learned and cooked numerous delicious dishes on the weekend. Often, Mom invited her students over, and Mom and Dì Út prepared the most delicious charbroil grilled beef-and-vegetable kabobs. I loved it when we had parties because Mom's students would spoil us with treats, and I enjoyed hearing happy chatting and laughter in our house.

Fast forward to 2017-2020: Mom had a stroke and was under intensive care for months in the hospital and later at a nursing home. Dì Út (who doesn't drive) took the bus to visit my mom daily. Mom's condition went up and down, and during her worst time, Dì Út constantly prayed by her bed and kept telling us that Mom would be OK. At the hospital and the nursing home, Dì Út was seen bugging all the nurses or doctors, constantly ensuring that Mom would get enough care and attention. It was Dì Út who was always talking to Mom, even in times when Mom was unconscious. And I'm telling you, even during the worst time, when Mom didn't recognize anyone except my dad and would not say anything to anybody, she would give a big smile when she saw Dì Út.

Dì Út took the bus to my parents' home several times a week for three years. She helped Mom with her bath and meals or pushed Mom around the neighborhood in her wheelchair. When Mom was with Dì Út, she was always smiling. For my mom, they were times of pain. But with Dì Út, she seemed happy again.

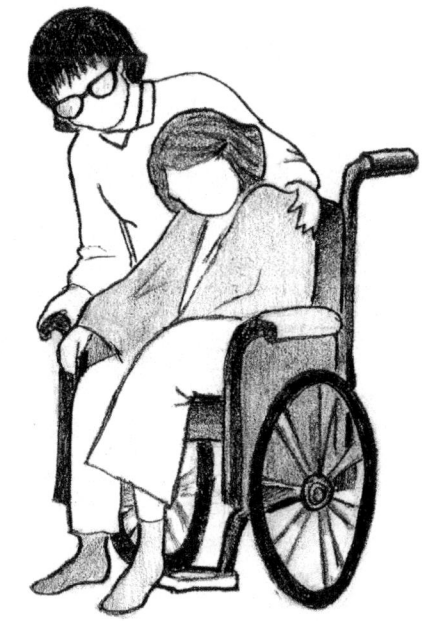

Mom – Mộng Hoàn

Mom was Grandpa and Grandma's third child, and she followed Grandma's example in arts. In 1960, Mom attended the University of Huế and joined the Society of Catholic University Students, and she met Dad here. During one of the university's camping trips, they got to know each other better.

Since Grandma hosted many meetings for the Society of Huế University's Catholic Students at her home, Dad often visited Mom's family. His family's heartbreaking story touched Grandma; she treated him as her own child. Grandma loved him dearly because she admired his excellent manner, independence, and honesty.

Life in Đà Nẵng

Mom and Dad fell in love, married, and built a family together in 1965. After graduating, Dad got a teaching job in Đà-Nẵng. In 1972, Dad became the principal of Đà Nẵng Tech School (Trường Kỹ Thuật Đà Nẵng), while Mom taught in several high schools in the city. She specialized in literature and writing.

Dad and Mom were wonderful teachers. Dad taught Math, Chemistry, and Physics, while Mom taught Literature. Their students loved them, and our house was always filled with students working on their school projects. To this day, many still remember them as great teachers and continue to visit or write to Dad. Before Mom passed away in 2020, their students often visited them in California.

In Đà Nẵng, our family lived happily and comfortably. During the day, Mom and Dad taught high school, and after dinner, Mom played the piano while my brother Tuyến, my sister Nu, and I did our homework.

A student of my parents came to our house every evening to tutor us. He was a kind and handsome young man who treated us with great respect. He once said that he hoped his future family would be as beautiful and loving as ours. Unbeknownst to us, this student was an undercover agent from the North Vietnamese government. His role was to monitor Dad's activities and report back to his supervisors in Hà Nội. In Đà Nẵng, Dad openly criticized communism, referencing the tragic experience of his parents and siblings who suffered under the communist regime. Given this, it wasn't surprising that he attracted the attention of the North Vietnamese government. Decades later, in the late 1990s, when Mom had a chance to meet this student again, he confessed that while spying on Dad, he had genuinely fallen in love with our family. When war erupted in Đà Nẵng in March 1975, he hurried to our house to ensure our safety. By the time he arrived, however, we had already departed for the port of Tiên Sa. I'll delve deeper into this story about the war in the next chapter.

Living with our family in Đà Nẵng were my grandpa, Uncle Huệ, Uncle Bê-Em, and Aunt Hoài. Our family was close-knit, and we enjoyed each other's company. Grandpa was very kind to us children and often gave us delicious snacks. We loved sitting on Grandpa's bed, reading our favorite comic books, while he sat close by, listening to his radio at a high volume. Whenever lively music played, he would stand up and dance joyfully. He swayed his hips, snapped his fingers, and tapped his foot to the beat. We laughed and had a great time watching him twist and move to the music, and sometimes, we even joined him in dancing.

Uncle Bê Em once built a treehouse for us in our backyard, where we played all the time. One day, my brother Tuyến told my sister Nu that if she held onto a chicken, she could "fly" from the treehouse to the ground.

Since Dad had plenty of chickens in the yard, my brother Tuyến and Nu decided to try this "flying" adventure with the chickens. Fortunately, they both landed on the ground without breaking any bones!

Dad also had two cows in our yard. These cows loved coming near our kitchen window. Their favorite treats were jackfruit peels. Whenever we opened jackfruits  in the kitchen, the cows would quickly gallop to the window, put their heads in, and moo loudly, demanding for their favorite snack.

 Our family usually went to church on the weekends and visited Grandma afterward. It was lovely when we had many relatives living nearby.

One of my favorite memories was our Tết celebration at Grandma's house. We all dressed in beautiful clothes and lined up to wish Grandpa and Grandma good health and prosperity. In return, they gave us red envelopes with brand-new money for good luck, a tradition called lì-xì.

During Tết, as we savored delicious treats, my siblings and I were happy to hang out with our cousins.

Our days were always filled with laughter. The rooms were filled with family and friends, and the sweet yet tangy aroma of food filled the air. We would find any reason to celebrate and come together to enjoy life.

Life was beautiful until 1975, when the North Vietnamese army attacked South Vietnam and changed everything.

Things were never the same again.

Chapter 4: War

Running from war

I watched Dad stare at a vase filled with yellow apricot flowers.

The bright petals slowly fell off the dying stem, and Dad seemed worried.

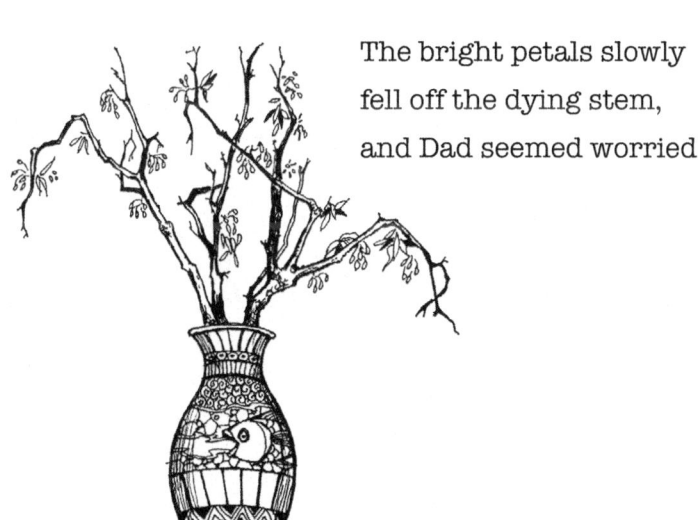

Dad looked at the refugees camping outside.

He said, "Remember when the communists came to Huế with a blacklist in 1968? They hunted down more than 5,000 people and rounded up those in the forest. They tied them in groups and buried them alive. These victims were government officers, teachers, priests, nuns, and other normal civilians like us. "I have been an anti-communist aggressively and openly in this city. Everyone who knows me can see that. I'm definitely on the communists' blacklist now. My father was executed for being a landowner. I'm sure that fact already made me the enemy of the Party. We need to get out of here before they catch us."

The whole family heeded the warning. Mom and Aunt Hoài hurriedly packed things into bags while Dad instructed us to each take one bag with our most important belongings.

Uncle Bê Em sewed Mom a cloth belt. Inside the belt, he hid a small stack of thin gold sheets, a small fortune Dad and Mom had been saving after years of hard work. He attached the belt to her pants to keep our family's gold fortune safe.

"It took us years to save up for this gold," Mom told Uncle Bê Em. "It must be around 40 ounces."

Uncle Bê Em replied, "You must take care of these pants. The whole family's fortune is now in your pants."

Dad and Uncle Huệ opened our safe, took all the cash, and stuffed the money into a small suitcase.

It was all moving so fast. Being only six, I couldn't fully grasp what was happening.

I asked Mom, "What's going on?"

Mom reached for the two pretty dolls displayed in a glass case and gave them to my sister Nu and me. They were kept in the display most of the time, and we could only play with them occasionally.

We are getting out of here. You kids take care of your dolls now.

As scared as I was, I was happy that I was allowed to hold the doll the whole time.

"Hurry!" Dad called.

We rushed into the car parked outside.

The journey to the city port usually took an hour, but due to heavy traffic, it took forever. I held onto my doll tightly, looking out the car window.

The streets were filled with people all heading in the same direction. I saw a whole family of five on a motorbike piled with bags. Some people pushed their luggage on their bicycles, and some walked. It was a scene of panic and chaos as everyone tried to escape.

When we reached Tien-Sa port, what I saw was surreal: Thousands of people, families young and old, gathered there seeking refuge. The tension was palpable, and everyone feared what was to come.

The crowd was so thick that moving the car further was impossible. Dad abandoned the vehicle, and we carried the bags on foot, trying to get closer to the dock. There, we found Grandma and our aunts Hài and Huyền.

I didn't fully understand what communists or Vietcong meant, but I could sense the danger. All I knew was that something profound and perilous was coming. I clutched the doll tightly and followed my family into the mass of people at the port.

We waited there all day.

Dad said that the Americans were ordered not to come in and help the Vietnamese. In a low voice, he told us that an American Navy ship had been waiting in the ocean near the dock. They wanted to help us, but every time the ship attempted to come closer, hidden communist spies shot at it from the shore. The American ship was not allowed to hit back.

Night fell, gunfire and explosions filled the air. The darkness felt endless, pressing down on us, amplifying every terrifying sound.

None of us ate or drank all day, but fear overpowered hunger.

Babies were crying, and people were wailing louder than I could imagine.

A madman was walking around, yelling and hitting people with his cane.

Everyone in my family gathered close to each other. The adults tried to sit in a protective circle with the children and Grandma in the middle so we wouldn't get hit or stepped on. We huddled together, praying for safety.

I was exhausted from the harrowing experiences of that day. Leaning on one of the bags, I finally fell asleep.

When I woke up, the sky turned from dark to silver.

The barge

A barge had docked at the port, and the sea of people swelled to meet it.

"We all need to move fast and get on it before it is full and too late," Dad said.

I heard kids crying and screaming as they searched for their parents. People were pushing one another. Some people fell. Many others stepped on them.

The adults in my family quickly gathered our belongings.

"Aunts and Uncles, each of you, please look over Má and one of the children," Dad said. "This crowd is too chaotic. Make sure they are safe with you."

As we were pulled toward the ship, I saw little children lying on the ground. I yelled at them, but they remained still.

"Those children are dead. Leave them. Let's go." Grandma said as she pulled my hand.

The crowd thrust us to the edge of the dock. Dad shouted at us to keep together as a group, but it felt impossible.

I saw people shove one another as they tried to jump on the barge. Some were pushed hard and fell into the water.

The barge kept slamming hard at the rocky dock. It crushed the people who fell.

I watched people in front of me hurrying over to the barge. I saw Dad jump behind Mom.

I jumped, too.

But I slipped and fell.

I grabbed the rail at the edge of the ferry and screamed.

Hold on tight!

Dad!

It was hard to believe that Dad heard me amid the crowd's noise. As he turned, I could see fear in his eyes.

Dad pulled me up just before the barge slammed hard against the dock. We turned to where Dad had thrown the suitcase, but it was no longer there.

We looked in the water and saw all our money floating in the rough waves of the sea.

Dad quickly turned away and pulled me deeper into the barge. The whole family was already there, huddling in one corner, waiting. The hot sun beat down on us.

As I gazed around, my eyes met with each family member. We briefly felt relieved after overcoming such fearful episodes, now surrounded by our loved ones. We had witnessed so many dead people over the past few days; this relative safety made us feel humble and fortunate. It was a miracle that everyone had made it here together.

Around me, lifeless bodies filled the ground on the dock, a scene that looked to be the outcome of a stampede. Injured individuals scattered across the barge as their moans and cries pierced the air. They were all pleading for help. Everyone seemed in pain and distressed.

"I'm hungry," my younger brother Lĩnh cried.

"I'm thirsty," I cried.

We did not have anything to eat or drink for two days. Beside me, my sister and oldest brother lay motionless.

Uncle Huệ told us that some American helicopters were trying to drop bags of food, drink, and other emergency supplies onto the barge. However, the communist spies from the shore were shooting at them, so the supplies were landing in the ocean.

I was so exhausted when night fell that I couldn't cry anymore. When I eventually slept, I was caught between fleeting moments of consciousness and vivid dreams.

In one recurring dream, I found myself back in my house in front of the refrigerator. A cold bottle of water awaited me when I opened the fridge door. But I woke up every time I reached out to grasp it.

I opened my eyes and saw Dad kneeling, looking down at me. He seemed sad and worried. His eyes were red. He looked pale, and his lips were dry and cracked.

He took some saliva from his mouth and put it in my mouth to moisten it. He did the same for my sister and my brothers.

Then, people in the family passed around a metal cup, and everyone took a sip. The liquid in the cup was yellow. I drank it as I was told. It was bitter and did not help my thirst.

"It was Uncle Hanh's piss," my brother Tuyến told me. At that moment, it didn't even faze me. After three days without water, I would drink anything!

I drifted off again. When I woke up, the barge looked like it was moving, and Dad was no longer around us.

Uncle Huệ was talking about my mom to the family.

"Sister Hoàn drank the ocean water. Too much salt. She is not herself. We need to keep an eye on her," he said.

I looked at Mom. She looked lost. She was nursing my baby brother Yên. I was sure he could not find any milk because he was crying.

Then, Mom put the baby down and removed her outer pants, the ones that Uncle Bê Em had sewed gold leaves onto.

"It's too hot!"

Uncle Bê Em hurriedly grabbed the pants. He removed a bottle from his Red Cross bag and splashed the reddish-looking liquid over them. It must have been a disinfecting solution. The pants now looked gross, as if they were stained with blood.

Somewhere nearby, I heard my grandma, aunts, and uncles saying their prayers softly. They also hummed church songs. They must have been exhausted since the sounds of prayers would stop and go. I repeatedly heard words: "Our Father, who art in heaven ... Holy Mary, full of grace ... Please have mercy on us ... Please pray for us now and at the hour of death ..."

I closed my eyes and listened to their whispering prayers; the prayers calmed me down. That was the last thing I could remember before I passed out.

I woke up feeling cool water splashing on my face. It was raining!

"RAIN!" I yelled out happily.

The first thought that came to my mind was that God had answered my grandmother's prayers! I lay there with my mouth wide open, letting the rain wet my tongue and throat. The rainwater tasted pure and sweet. The best drink ever!

Eventually, I tried to sit up. Something heavy was on top of my stomach. Looking down, I was terrified to see a big body whose massive head was on my belly! I tried to wiggle. It took me a while to pull myself free of that big load.

Finally, I could stand up and look down at that body. The face looked gray and purple. It was a dead body! No matter how often I saw one, I could never get used to it.

I walked away from the corpse and looked around. People had hung up plastic tarps to make shelters from the rain—puddles of rainwater collected on the tarps. After days with nothing to drink, they looked delicious! I pulled on one corner of a tarp and let the cool, fresh water run down my parched lips and scratchy throat. It tasted so good!

I felt hazy as I wandered around, trying to remember who or where I was! Then, I heard someone call my name. I turned around. It was my sister Nu walking towards me. My memories suddenly returned. I remembered that we were on a barge, and I had thought we would all die!

I smiled at Nu. She looked happy to see me, too.

Why are you naked?

I looked down, stunned. Nu was right. I had nothing on!

Nu dug through the dead bodies of the children around us. She found a white shirt, and I put it on.

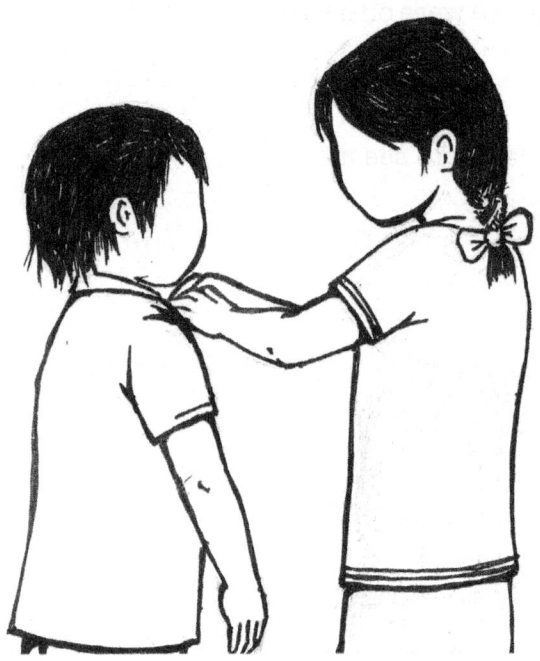

"The label on the shirt is from another school, not ours. You should wear it inside out so people won't know we took it from someone else," Nu suggested.

The rain stopped. We walked around the barge to look for our family. I must have been still in shock since I felt like I was walking around without feelings or thoughts. It was like a thick glass wall separating me from everything around me. I looked at dead bodies but felt no fear. I observed people crying and distressed, but it stirred no emotions in me.

The barge was packed with people sitting and lying about. As we made our way across the barge, we had to step over dead bodies piled on top of each other.

I noticed a girl about 14 years old holding a baby, and next to her was a little girl. A boy about three years old was sitting in a basket at her feet. The little kids were crying. I didn't see their parents.

We found our family huddled up together. They were happy to see us. Dad embraced both of us tight, tears in his eyes. Dad told us that, for a short while, he had lost his mind, too.

He had wandered around the barge with no memories of his family. He thought he was still living in North Vietnam during the Land Reform time and that the communists were putting him on trial. He had been so scared that he almost jumped off the barge to run away from the communists. Then he saw Mom and Grandma. That was when he woke up from his delusion.

I looked around and smiled at the family, seeing that every one of us was there.

The American ship

Suddenly, I felt a surge in the crowd, and people started to get up.

An American ship came towering over us. Everyone ran toward it.

Dad said the crowd would fight each other to board the Navy ship. The crowd could be dangerous, especially to children and older people. Again, he wanted us to watch out for one another.

"We need to ensure that no one would be left behind, stepped on by the crowd, or pushed into the ocean by accident," Dad said.

"This will help our family to survive for a while."

Dad also told Uncle Bê Em to hold on tight to Mom's pants, which Uncle Bê Em had poured the red liquid on. Now that he had lost the suitcase with the cash inside, the 40 oz. of gold hidden in Mom's pants was all we had left.

My family moved toward the ship as a pack while I held on tight to Aunt Hoài.

People climbed rope ladders to get to the ship from the barge. They looked like tiny ants crawling on top of one another to reach the colony.

Mom looked up at the American ship, still dazed. She looked around and found a basket. She put baby Yên in it and gave the basket to the man beside her.

I was sure she had not yet recovered from drinking the ocean water, which made her act oddly.

Dad pushed people aside and stepped up, taking my baby brother from Mom and helping Mom get closer to the ship.

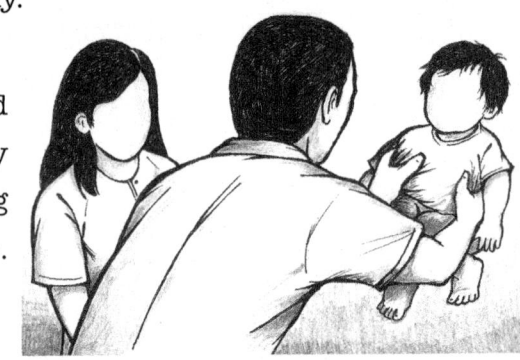

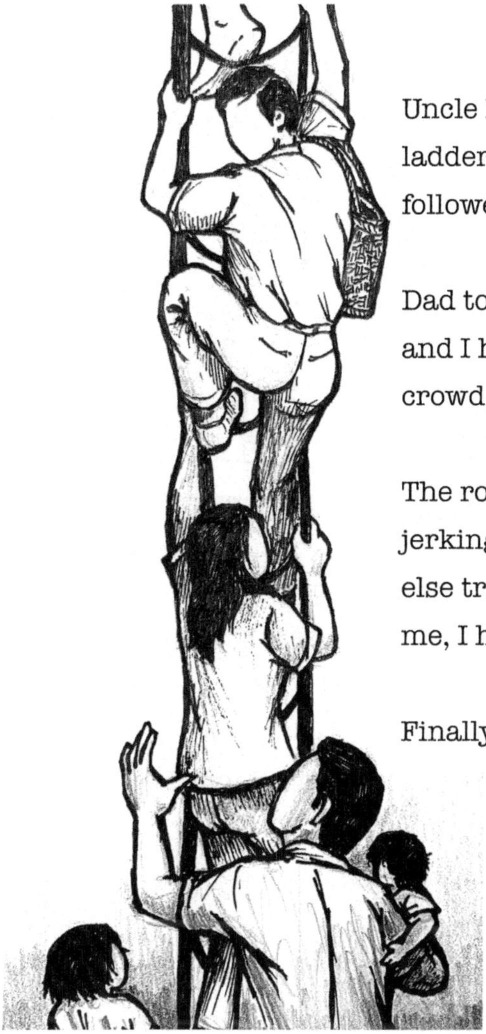

Uncle Bê Em grabbed the rope ladder and started to climb; Mom followed him.

Dad told me to climb before Dad, and I heard him shout over the crowd, "Hold on tight!"

The rope swung back and forth, jerking violently whenever someone else tried to climb on it. As Dad told me, I held on to it tightly.

Finally, I reached the top.

Once aboard, we were pushed aside by a group of South Vietnamese marines who directed people to move further into the ship. It was packed.

A Vietnamese man in a marine outfit was searching Mom. He said he had to make sure no one was carrying a weapon. He finally let her pass after she gave him her gold wedding ring. Mom seemed to be much better and not as deranged as before.

The marine also stopped Uncle Bê Em to search his body. Uncle Bê Em held up the bloody-looking pants and pointed at Mom. "It's my sister's pants. She's having her period." The man seemed disgusted and let Uncle Bê Em pass. That was how our family gold was safe from being robbed. These gold leaves would help our big family survive the next ten years.

Uncle Huệ was standing nearby. He waved me over and told me to stand beside my grandma and aunt Hài in the corner, away from the ship's edge. My older brother Tuyến and my sister Nu were there also.

I saw Dad emerge with my baby brother. As soon as Dad got up, he gave baby Yên to Uncle Huệ and tried to climb down again. He said he needed to help Aunt Huyền, who waited at the other end of the robe to bring my younger brother Lĩnh up. However, a marine stopped him. Dad took off his gold wedding band and gave it to the soldier, and he let Dad go.

Finally, our family was together in one group again. By some miracle, we did not miss anyone. Grandma told us to thank God for protecting us throughout the horrible days.

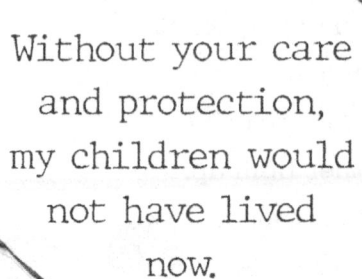

"Without your care and protection, my children would not have lived now."

Dad thanked my uncles and aunts for protecting us children.

We sat leaning against a metal rail. The Vietnamese marines gave people bags of instant rice soaked in water. The rice tasted spongy and smelled like plastic. However, I was so hungry that I ate a spoonful or two.

Then I saw the girl whom I had seen on the ferry earlier. But the baby, the younger girl, and the little boy were not with her this time. I had no idea what had happened to them. The girl sat quietly alone, her gaze fixed on something far away. I wasn't sure if she was exhausted or frightened, or both.

Dad gestured for us to look at the ship's bridge. The American officers stood inside the glass window, looking down at the deck filled with people.

Dad overheard the South Vietnamese marines say that the communists promised to hold fire until the Americans left the city. Also, by this agreement, the Americans were to withdraw from Vietnam immediately and were not supposed to get involved with the war between the North and South Vietnamese. However, the ship's captain and the officers felt they couldn't leave the war refugees scrambling to run away from the communists, so they locked themselves in the cabin and let the South Vietnamese conduct the rescue process.

"Hah! And that rescuing process sure includes the robbing from the civilians also," Uncle Bê Em said sarcastically.

Dad nodded in agreement.

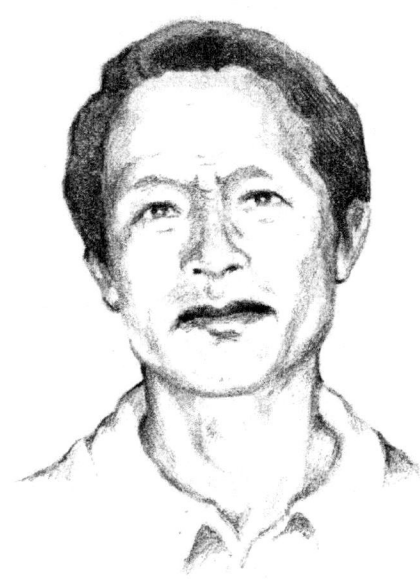

Then Dad said, "This ship will bring us further to the south, where the South Vietnamese army still stands. We will get off at one of the ports at Cam-Ranh. From there, we will find our way to get to Saigon. Maybe by bus."

I looked up at Dad. He was gazing at the horizon toward the north, yet his mind seemed far away. His eyes were dark as the sky before a storm; I wasn't sure if they were filled with worries or sorrow.

"I'm not sure how long we can be safe in the south until they catch up to us again," Dad whispered.

As the ship sailed farther from our home, thoughts of the vibrant, yellow apricot flowers filled my mind. The yellow apricot flowers permeated our living room with a fragrance in the morning when I woke and excitedly dressed up for Tết, the Vietnamese New Year.

Then, I remembered the tiny petals falling on the ground while Dad tended to the branches. I found those thoughts drifting away as I lost sight of the shore.

But then I looked over at my family to see everyone here. Our home was lost, yet we were all together, and that was all that truly mattered.

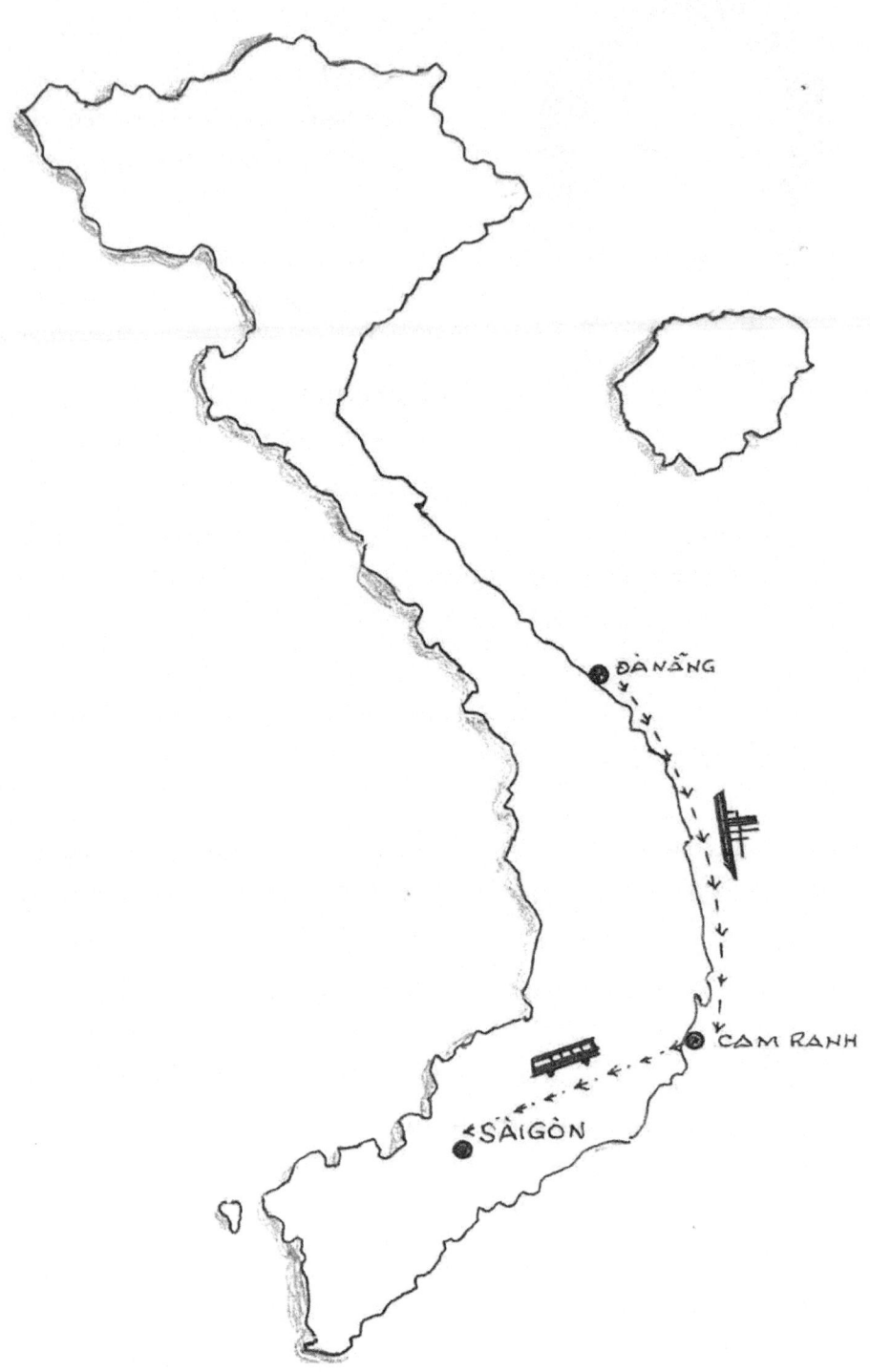

Chapter 5: Living in the Exile

Unknown Future

When we arrived in Sài-Gòn, Dad's friend let us stay in his house until we could figure out what to do next.

That house was a pleasant home spacious enough to accommodate our large extended family.

Then, in late April 1975, things started to become chaotic again. We heard gunshots and explosions every day.

Our family watched the fall of the South Vietnamese government and feared the nightmares of the approaching North Vietnamese taking over the country.

Having witnessed the murder of his parents by the communist government in the 1950s and the bloody massacre in Hue by the North Vietnamese army, Dad knew our future with the new regime would be very grim.

I often pretended to sleep and listened to my parents whispering at night. Once, I heard Dad say, "A student of mine warned me that I'm on the blacklist. They know I'm a very active anti-communist. And with my family history, if I get caught, they'll kill me."

He sounded scared. I was scared. Our world would be gone if they found Dad.

However, Dad came up with a plan.

The following day, I heard my parents whisper while my siblings and I looked through an old comic book we found in the house. Dad told Mom that we needed to go into hiding and that we needed to leave soon.

"Where will we go?" Mom asked.

"I learned from childhood that if we have some land, we can grow food and won't be starving. I'll look for a quiet place further down south, far from here. No one will know who we are," Dad replied.

Thank God we still have the gold. That will help us to survive a while.

Everything was moving so fast. My mind was filled with questions and confusion, but I was not allowed to speak. I was not allowed to know anything.

Then, Dad was gone for a while.

Mom told Grandma that someone had told Dad about a nearly deserted area near the southwest border. He decided to go check it out.

"There are only few farmers living in that area. And most of them speak Khmer. He will change his name, and we will all live there. We will be safe," said Mom.

Going into hiding

Every day, I sat by the window, worried about Dad. Was he safe? When will he be back? When it rained at night, I thought of him being alone in a strange place, wet and cold.

When Dad returned, our family packed up our meager belongings. According to Dad, we were heading southwest to a province called Takeo, near a small town named Rạch Giá. Our family would go first, and then, once we were settled, Grandma and my aunts and uncles would join us.

Dad took us to a large bus depot, where vehicles of all sizes were crammed next to each other. It took a lot of work to figure out which bus was supposed to go where. At a wooden table with a handwritten sign reading "Ticket Counter," a man told us all the bus tickets were sold out. However, someone tipped Dad off on how to get the tickets on the "black market." Indeed, we found men and women walking around discreetly selling seats on their buses at much higher prices.

There was so much noise at the bus depot. Street vendors shouted, trying to sell food and merchandise—from coconut candies and dumplings to woven straw tote bags and cone hats made of coconut leaves. Young children dressed in rags wandered around, selling cigarettes from small wooden boxes that hung from their necks. Some begged us to buy their goods; others just begged for change. They all looked skinny and hungry.

Dad was trying to decide which bus we should take. The small buses, powered by coal burning in the metal cylinder barrel at the rear of these rustic vehicles, offered cheaper fares. Nevertheless, they moved slowly. Additionally, the coal would make the ride boiling hot during the scorching summer weather.

Finally, Dad found us tickets to ride on one of the old diesel-fueled buses, hoping it would get us to Rạch Giá before dark. We walked to the bus and looked up. It looked big and rustic, and it smelled like fuel and sweat. Many people sat on the bus's roof, holding onto their bicycles, baskets, and bags.

The bus was already jammed with people, tightly packed like sardines, with piles of bags on the floor under their feet. We tried to squeeze in, but since there were no more seats, the driver told us to sit in the aisle on top of the piles of luggage.

Three ducks stuck their heads out of a basket under the seat next to me. They kept poking at the bag I was sitting on. I think they were looking for food.

Mom was holding my baby brother Yên, and someone let Mom sit at the edge of a bench.

Dad stood next to Mom, holding onto the rail near the door. It was open the whole time, even when the bus was running. At Dad's feet, a pig grunted nonstop and smelled terrible.

We were trapped inside the bus in the sweltering heat. The body odor from the tightly packed people made me feel like I could faint. I needed air.

Fortunately, the bus started moving, and some cool air blew in.

The road was bumpy, and the bus rumbled and shook when it ran. A man stood by the open door, hanging his body halfway outside the bus. He banged fiercely on its side and yelled at the crowd.

"Move! Make way!"

His yelling helped push the crowd back just enough for the bus to move forward

Soon, we were out of the city. Craning my neck to look out the window, I saw fields of green vegetables and tiny houses with tin roofs passing by. There were also many palm trees and banana trees. That was the first time I had seen places other than cities. The scenery was peaceful and quiet.

The bus occasionally stopped to let people off and pick up more passengers. Local people came near the bus during the stops, trying to sell food, snacks, and fruits through the open windows. We were hungry, and I hoped Mom would buy us some yummy treats, but she handed us some rice balls that she had pressed earlier that morning. We ate them sprinkled with salt and roasted sesame seeds.

When we arrived at a little town called Rạch-Giá, it was almost sunset. We got off the bus and walked to a dock where Dad hired a man to take us on a river in his small boat. I had never seen a river or a boat in real life before.

Children nearby stared at us as if we were from another planet. Even the adults looked at us with great curiosity. Dressed like city people, we sure looked different from the locals.

We gingerly stepped on the tiny boat, which bobbed with every step. We sat on the wet, muddy wooden planks that lined the bottom of the canoe. The little engine rumbled, and the canoe lurched so violently that I fell backward onto my younger brother Lĩnh, sitting behind me. Like me, my siblings were in awe of the new things surrounding us.

The riversides were lined with thick plants that Dad called mangroves. They looked like palm trees, but they grew in water. Mosquitoes hovered in a dense cloud above the water, and we started itching on our arms and necks.

I stuck my arm out and scooped up some water. It felt warm and looked thick with light golden specks in the sunlight at the end of the day.

"The river carries rich sediments in the water, which provides nutrients for the plants grown on the farms," Dad explained.

We finally arrived at a vast open field, and
the man and his boat left. Now, it was only us
in the dark.

As we huddled together at the expanse that
was supposed to be our land, we listened
to the hum of insects, the croaks of frogs,
the chirps of nightbirds, and the clicks and
whistles of other unidentified animals. No
one was around for miles except maybe a few
families of farmers and fishermen.

I looked at Dad, who gestured for us to follow him further inland.

This land was called Tà Keo. Here, Dad stripped away his individuality and possessed a new, completely different identity. He had to pretend to be a farmer who barely knew how to read and write. My dad was the most intelligent, social, educated, and intellectual person I knew. How would he pretend to be someone he is not?

Adjusting to the New Life

Before bringing us here, Dad and some local farmers he hired built a house for us. They used raw materials like bamboo and eucalyptus trees for the frame and made a thatched roof out of palm leaves and straw. The house stood tall and alone in the empty field.

The house was built to fit everyone, including my grandma and Mom's siblings.

The interior of the house was one long room. Standing on one end, one could see the other end. Our bamboo beds were lined up one after another along the side walls. The only furniture in our house was a long bamboo dining table with two long eucalyptus wood benches on both sides.

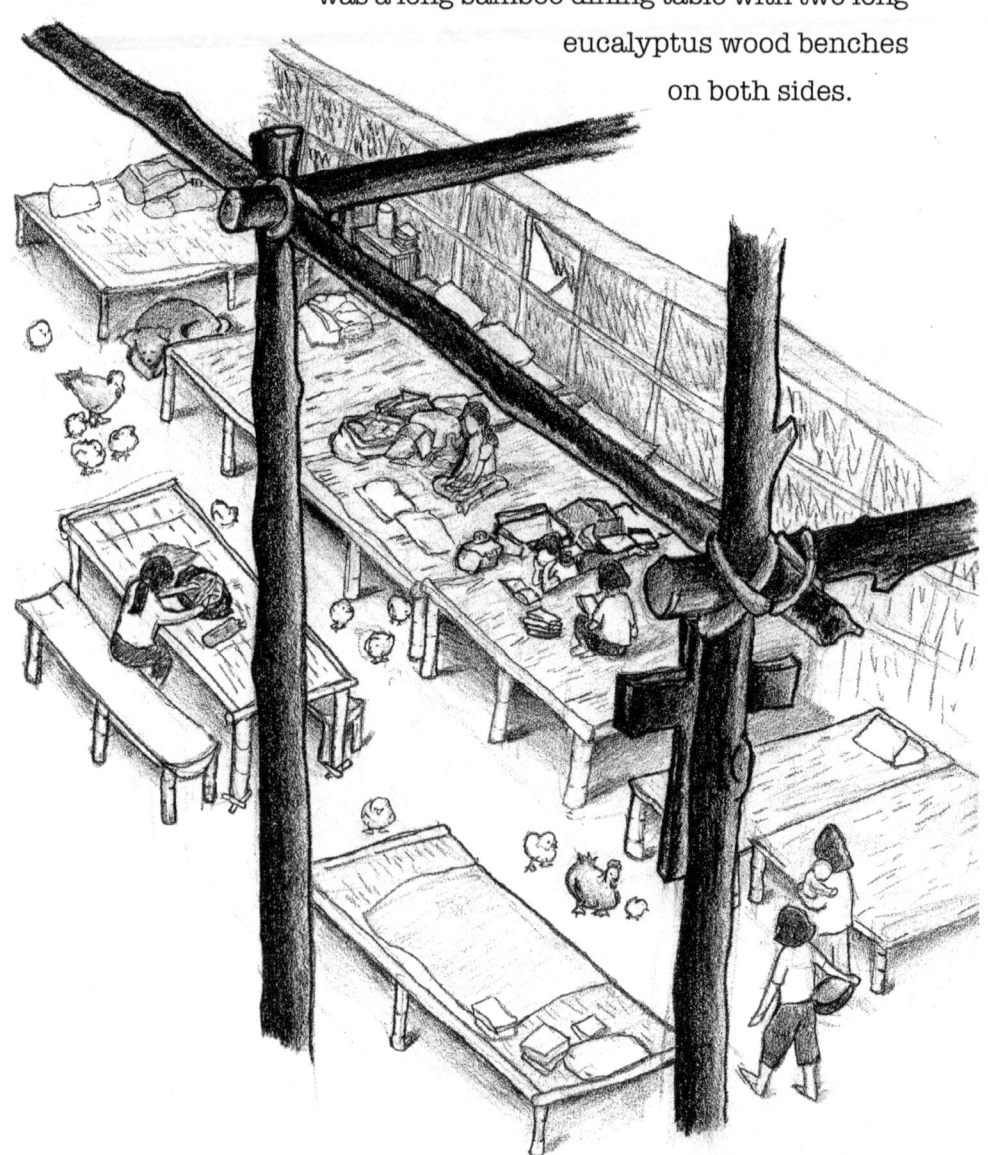

At night, the table was turned into a bed for my sister Nu and me.

When the locals rode their boats nearby, they flashed their broad smiles at us, their teeth sparkly white against their ebony skin. Though they were curious about how different we looked, they often left us alone. When they did speak to us, it was in their Khmer dialect.

Hah! Your house is too tall! The wind will blow it down!

The locals were right. Very often, a storm would come. The wind blew violently against our house, making the walls sway back and forth.

My siblings and I huddled up together in our parents' bed and trembled.

"The house is collapsing!"

One storm brought so much rain that it flooded the house. Dad and my uncles chopped down eucalyptus trees to build bridges so we could walk inside. Most of the time, my siblings and I hopped from one bed to another. When we saw fish and eels swimming under our beds, my oldest brother Tuyen tried to catch a fish with a tin can.

There is water all over anyway, so what's the difference?

It was not convenient to take the little kids out to go to the bathroom. So, Aunt Huyền told my little brother Lĩnh to pee out the window whenever he needed to go.

Wild and free time

Months passed, and Dad adjusted to his new lifestyle. As I sat in our yard every morning, I watched him leave for the field, where he would grow rice, watermelons, sugar canes, and sweet potatoes. Sometimes, he showed us how to chop wood so the family could use it to cook our meals.

Mom was pregnant with my youngest sister, Nhon, and was getting heavier daily. While Dad was busy making a living for us and Mom was getting increasingly tired, my siblings, cousins, and I roamed free in the rice fields.

The most fun was when Mom's older sister, Aunt Hoà, and her family came to stay with us. Her six children, Ti, Tuấn, Tín, Toàn, Tân, and Tiến, were all around the same age as my siblings and me.

Later, Mom's younger sister Hằng sent her daughter Tri-Túc to visit us. She was happy to join our gang.

From morning to night, we all played together. We would find bamboo and paper to make kites. Without toys, we would spend hours digging clay to make our own figurines. We roamed the fields under the scorching sun.

Of course, we also argued and fought a lot about everything! However, if the boys hit one another when they fought, Aunt Hoà would ask them to shake hands to make peace.

Playing in the hay all day made us all itchy, so we would jump in the river to cool off.

Our dog Xay-nai swam with us.

Xay-nai was part of our pack. I still remember when my uncle Hậu brought home this little brown furball of a puppy. His color resembled milk coffee, so my uncle named him Xay-nai, which meant "Milk Coffee" in the local dialect.

"He is so furry; people wouldn't steal him to cook him up for dinner. They believed eating a furry dog would cause them hives!" Uncle Hậu reasoned.

A herd of water buffaloes would often swim by us when we swam. I was excited to see the buffaloes and scared at the same time. These creatures looked big and imposing with their massive pointed horns.

We would always try to count how many there were, sometimes as many as a dozen. A boy usually sat on the back of the first buffalo, and another sat on the last. If any buffalo trailed off, one of the boys would holler at the buffaloes and gently hit the one that trailed off with the tip of a bamboo branch. That buffalo would obediently turn and follow the herd.

Although it was exciting to see water buffaloes, we quickly learned they carried leeches whenever they swam by. Once we saw them approach our way, we would rush to get out of the river. One time, my cousin Toàn couldn't get out fast enough. Leeches filled his legs. We ran to Mom, screaming for help. She told us to sprinkle salt over his legs; it worked amazingly! The leeches melted off.

Learning to sustain ourselves

With such a large family and little money for food. Uncle Hậu suggested we catch mice to enhance our dinner.

One afternoon, Uncle Hậu took us children and our dog, Xay-nai, to the middle of the field. He gathered us in a circle and told us we would learn to catch the mice ourselves. I was astonished.

First, Uncle Hậu walked around the field in a circle, burning the dry hay on the ground. Then, he hit the ground hard with a stick. Seeing what he did, we all joined him, running behind him in a circle with sticks we found on the ground. We hit the ground and made a lot of noise by yelling loudly. Soon enough, I saw a mouse peek out from a small hole in the middle of the circle.

"Mice!" my brother yelled.

The more we stomped, the more mice emerged and ran to the middle of the circle. Xay-nai also excitedly circled the perimeter, barking loudly.

"Everybody close in!" Uncle Hậu shouted.

We slowly entered the middle of the circle, catching the mice with bags, pots, and pans. It was exhilarating.

Afterward, Uncle Hậu showed us how to skin the mice, clean the guts, and grill them over an open fire. We all gathered around and devoured every last bite. They were delicious.

After we learned how to hunt for mice, we eventually learned how to catch snakes, fish and frogs.

Everybody had a job.

In addition to hunting for food, all the kids had to help with chores like picking herbs and vegetables or paddling our little boat to the market to buy essentials.

I was responsible for boiling the water fetched from the river. Once cooled, I filtered the water through a cloth to remove the brownish sediment, resulting in less bitter-tasting drinking water.

We were also learning, and Aunt Huyền homeschooled us. Aunt Huyền was merely 21 years old and looked gorgeous. She was also brilliant. She taught us basic cursive writing and math.

At night, after dinner, we gathered around her on our beds, listening to her stories. We didn't have any books, so we relied on her to learn about all the legends and historical fiction she had learned in high school. Our childhood dreams were based on all the tales we heard from Aunt Huyền. When she ran out of stories from books, she told stories of the movies she had seen, and when she ran out of that, she told us romantic stories about all the boys who fussed over her when she was still in high school. She was a great storyteller, and though we live thousands of miles apart now, we still feel a close bond with her that will never fade.

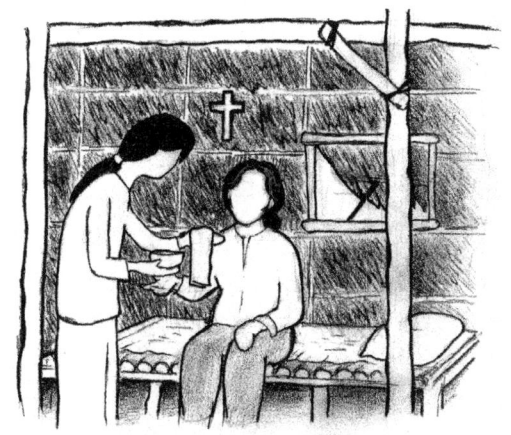

Our other aunt, Aunt Hài, was in charge of caring for Grandma. She was always beside Grandma. Everything Grandma needed would be at her fingertips, thanks to Aunt Hài. She brought water and a moist towel to Grandma in the morning when Grandma was up. She then made breakfast and tea and set them at Grandma's bedside table. She ensured that Grandma ate, drank, and slept enough. She also helped manage the little money that Grandma made from drawing portraits of the farmers and their wives.

Grandma was very popular with the locals. The farmers asked her to draw their portraits so that their children could use these pictures to worship them after their passing, a Vietnamese tradition. The farmers were pleased with her work. Grandma drew them looking pretty and posh, dressed in nice suits and dresses adorned with sparkling jewels. They were so proud. Since they were poor, as payment, instead of money, they brought us fish, rice, and vegetables collected from their fields.

When Grandma was not busy drawing, she taught us how to draw. She was my first art teacher. Thanks to her, I fell in love with what I saw around me. She taught me to recognize beauty in simple, ordinary things, and I have never stopped drawing since.

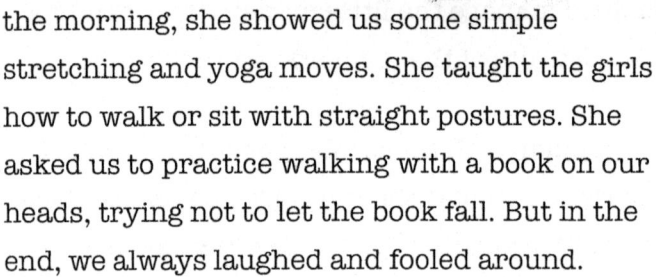

Grandma also encouraged us to exercise. In the morning, she showed us some simple stretching and yoga moves. She taught the girls how to walk or sit with straight postures. She asked us to practice walking with a book on our heads, trying not to let the book fall. But in the end, we always laughed and fooled around.

Grandma took us to walk around the fields when we were bored with lessons. She would carry a small sickle to cut dry branches from wild banana trees. We were supposed to collect them to bring home so our family could use them to make fires to cook our meals.

My youngest aunt, Dì Út (Aunt Hoài), was a fantastic cook. She had a talent for creating delicious meals from our limited food supply.

The river near our house led to the ocean, which affected the tides. The river rose and receded twice daily, which was how often Aunt Dì Út got into the kitchen to cook for our family of 15 people or more. Sometimes, when relatives visited and stayed, the family grew to more than two dozen!

Dì Út also loved music, sentimental songs, and romantic poems. Dì Út would encourage us to sing when not working in the kitchen. Her voice was gentle and sweet. Thanks to her, I learned to sing all the famous love songs that started my love for music. Dì Út would also show us how to create our own music and poems.

When we came up with something new, we would sing it to each other. Those tender moments make me happy whenever I look back to my childhood.

Memories from this time weren't always fun and peaceful. The communist government, newly in power, banned anything culturally associated with the previous regime. Art, music, literature, and games cherished by the South Vietnamese people before April 1975 were deemed indecent, debaucherous, and immoral.

Once, during Tết (Vietnamese New Year), our family gathered to exchange traditional greetings and enjoy special New Year treats. We decided to play cards, a traditional activity during Tet, unaware that gambling was prohibited. While everyone in the family was happily engaged in conversation and laughter, two guards in uniforms, reeking of alcohol and appearing intoxicated, barged in. They claimed to be patrolling and accused us of gambling, commanding us to stop and threatening a fine.

My ten-year-old brother Tuyến bravely spoke up, "But it's Tết. Our family only wants to have some fun." In response, one of the guards pulled out his gun, aimed it at Tuyến's head, and menacingly yelled, "Shut your mouth, or I'll blow your head off!"

Fear gripped me. Mom and Dad knelt, pleading for forgiveness; they offered the meager cash we had to make them leave. Since that incident, the sight of anyone with a gun would instill in me a trembling fear.

The lack of food, harsh living conditions, and uncertain futures made those days difficult. However, Mom kept our spirits up with her optimism. She believed we could handle anything and that tomorrow would always be better. She used to say, "God will take care of us. There's no need to fear."

Mom loved organizing music nights for us, and Aunt Huyền taught us how to dance to the lyrics of Uncle Huệ's songs. We would also sing songs, recite poems, and play guitars together. Everyone would applaud.

Music was a source of joy and optimism for us, even though we lived in impoverished conditions. Music and being together helped us stay happy and hopeful.

Gradually, everything started falling into place. We began adapting to our new way of living—learning to walk on wet clay without slipping, digging holes in the field when we needed to relieve ourselves, and shaking out our bed mats each night to make sure they were free of critters before lying down.

Even today, I vividly recall the beautiful memories from those years despite the scarcity and hunger. I cherished the pure, fresh air; the nights adorned with a sky full of stars and a radiant moon; the captivating sunrises and sunsets that always bore a unique charm; the verdant, lush fields bordered by evergreen bamboo and banana trees; and the serene sight of water buffaloes grazing as young boys guided them.

I recall that every night, before sleep, Uncle Huệ would ask everyone in the family to gather for prayer together. We recited rosaries, read passages from the Bible, and sang hymns.

Above all, I remember the profound sense of belonging when the children squeezed in on one bed to talk at night. The cramped space of the bed never seemed to matter; all I remember was the warmth of being united as a family under one roof.

Surrounded by my family, the prayers before bedtime made me feel secure and comforted. Our faith helped us transcend our challenging circumstances, nurturing our hope for a better future.

Chapter 6: Dad's Siblings

Two unexpected guests

One afternoon in Tà-Keo, our family was happy to see two wonderful visitors: Dad's two brothers, Thuỵ and Lĩnh. The last time Dad saw them, Uncle Thuỵ was ten years old, and Uncle Lĩnh was barely 4. After over 20 years of being apart due to a long and bloody war, their reunion felt like a miracle.

They were so happy to hold each other in their arms. When the three brothers took turns trading stories to catch up for lost time, Uncles Thuỵ and Lĩnh shared with us what happened to Dad's siblings after he escaped North Vietnam in 1958.

Horrific times

In 1953, my grandfather, Hồ Châu, was unfairly put on trial and killed because he was wealthy and owned land. This left my grandmother to care for her four young children and her elderly mother-in-law. Aunt Mỹ was 11 years old, Uncle Thuỵ was 8, Aunt Miều was 5, and Uncle Lĩnh was only 2. They were forced out of their home and lived in a falling-apart shack at the edge of the village. It had previously been used to keep cattle.

Grandmother and Grandfather also had three grown daughters, all married with kids, living in nearby villages. These daughters couldn't help their mother because of the restrictive local authorities. They were banned from contacting their parents since their father was labeled as "the enemy of the People." The daughters' families were also accused of being "landowners" and had their belongings taken away. Although they weren't executed, their situation was no better than their mother's.

Aunt Miều still remembers this time. In 1953, on the day before the authorities came to tie her father up for the trial, Aunt Miều saw him lying alone on the front porch. To the 4-year-old girl, he appeared quiet, sad, and lonely. Then, large groups of people arrived to take him away. People also sealed the house, forcing the rest of the family to move out.

Aunt Miều watched people search her mother to ensure she wasn't hiding anything. Her mother was dressed in an *áo yếm* (a traditional women's undergarment) beneath a blouse, with a long skirt beneath a shorter skirt. This was a typical outfit at the time. The people repeatedly asked my grandmother to remove the layers of clothing. Eventually, they allowed her to keep one skirt and took the shorter one as the "property of the People."

Grandma felt helpless as she watched her young children and mother-in-law endure hunger day after day. Her own health deteriorated rapidly from malnutrition, leaving her so weak she could barely stand. But one day, with what little strength she had left, she dragged herself to a nearby village to visit her sister. When her sister Hà secretly slipped her a potatoe for the children, Grandma hid it under her clothes and began the long walk home. Before she could make it back, village guards stopped her. They searched her, found the potatoe, and in front of the entire village, shamed her as "a thief who stole from the People" — then confiscated the food she had fought so hard to bring home.

On other occasions, Grandmother ventured to the market, hoping to find a way to earn a little money to feed her family. People avoided her because they feared the authorities, so she returned empty-handed. Realizing that as long as she remained alive, no one would dare aid her family, Grandma made the heartbreaking decision to end her life—hoping that without her, her children might stand a better chance of survival.

Aunt Mỹ remembers the night in 1955 when her mother quietly prepared to end her life. That evening, she asked her son, Thuỵ, if he had a drawstring she could use. Their grandmother had warned Thuỵ that their mother might be struggling with suicidal thoughts, so he told her he didn't have one.

The night was hot and humid, and Aunt Mỹ couldn't sleep. Worry gnawed at her as she kept a quiet, watchful eye on their mother. She noticed her staying up unusually late, moving slowly through their run-down shack, putting things in order.

After struggling to stay awake for hours, Aunt Mỹ finally drifted off. Just before dawn, she woke to find her mother missing from the shack. Panic surged through her as she ran outside, tears streaming down her face. She called out and asking anyone she passed if they'd seen her mother.

Then—she heard a scream near the village well.

They found her mother at the bottom.

Villagers and distant relatives came together to pull her body out, lifting her gently from the water and wrapping her in an old straw mat. They laid her to rest beneath a mound of dirt at the village's edge, the earth still soft from the night.

Aunt Mỹ and her younger siblings stood by in shock, frozen. Grief weighed so heavily on their hearts that they could not even cry.

Uncle Lĩnh

After their mother passed away, Aunt Mỹ, along with her younger siblings Thuỵ and Miều, searched the landfill near their village's market for scraps of food. During bitter winter days, the children dug in the fields, hoping to find any small potatoes left behind after harvest.

Little Uncle Lĩnh, four years old at the time, stayed home with their elderly grandmother, who was sick from starvation. One day, when the three children returned home after scavenging, they could not find Lĩnh in their shack.

They desperately combed the area, reaching its edge where a river flowed. To get to the neighboring village, they had to cross a narrow makeshift bridge made of bamboo, called a *cầu khỉ* (monkey bridge); it was named so probably because it required the agility of a monkey to cross. The bridge was slippery, spanning the turbulent water below.

They rushed to their older sister, Aunt Thiệu, to report their lost four-year-old brother. And there they saw Uncle Lĩnh. Somehow, he had found his way to his sister's house.

How had he managed it? How did he know the way? He was only a baby; how did he cross the slippery monkey bridge? The only explanation they could fathom was that their parents hadn't left them; they were always there to shield them from harm.

Uncle Lĩnh stayed with Aunt Thiệu, who had to chop wood for a meager income in the forest during the day. She would leave Uncle Lĩnh at home, and each day, upon returning, she would find him tied to a pole. The village children would cruelly mimic the trials against landowners, subjecting him to daily torment. Due to malnutrition and repeated abuse, Uncle Lĩnh fell seriously ill. His body swelled, and he suffered from chronic diarrhea. His sister feared for his life.

Fortunately, a poor farmer named Nguỵ came to rescue Uncle Lĩnh. In his dream, Mr. Nguỵ was told he would be blessed with a son if he adopted an orphan. Childless and seeking blessings, he offered Aunt Thiệu five coins and took Uncle Lĩnh home. Every day, Mr. Nguỵ would take Uncle Lĩnh with him when he tended the cows on the field. Lĩnh's swollen body made walking difficult, and he often lost his balance. Once, he fell and rolled into a field. A nearby pedestrian pulled him up using a cotton sack. This man advised Mr. Nguỵ to search for a particular root, brew it into tea, and give it to Uncle Lĩnh to drink. Incredibly, the tea reduced the swelling, leading to Uncle Lĩnh's recovery.

Eventually, Mr. Nguỵ did have a son. Uncle Lĩnh continued to live with the family. He helped care for the infant when the baby was young. When the boy was a bit older, Uncle Lĩnh contributed to the fieldwork, tending the buffaloes and harvesting the crops.

As he became a young man, he shared the work with Mr. Nguỵ to make a meager living for the family. Very frequently, Uncle Lĩnh and Mr. Nguỵ carried loads of clay pots to the market to earn a modest income.

Despite enduring poverty, Uncle Lĩnh was grateful to have a family who cared for him.

Aunt Mỹ

After Mr. Nguy adopted Uncle Lĩnh, Aunt Mỹ continued to beg for discarded food at the village market. One day, Aunt Mỹ encountered a woman who was seeking a helper. This woman owned a textile shop and promised Aunt Mỹ the chance to attend school if she came to work for her. At 13 years old, having completed only fourth grade, Aunt Mỹ accepted the offer. She was excited to hear she could go to school again.

Aunt Mỹ had to work hard to stay at the woman's place. Her daily routine started at 3 a.m., when she walked six miles to the market, bearing a heavy load on her shoulder, overfilled with textile rolls. After delivering the loads at the shop, she hurriedly returned to school. After school, she assisted with countless household chores. A year later, the woman asked Aunt Mỹ to quit school for more work. Though disappointed, Aunt Mỹ complied to secure a place to stay. She worked at the woman's house for many years.

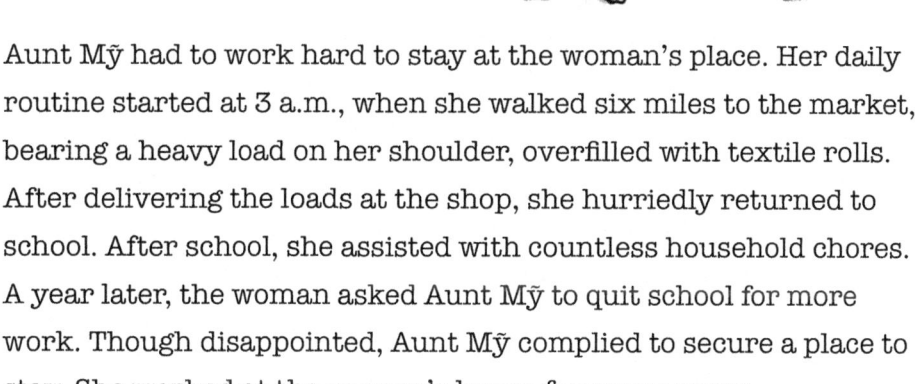

At 17, Mỹ's oldest sister, Aunt Thiệu, suggested that Aunt Mỹ should come back home to live with either sister Tiệu or Tạo, both with young children and needing assistance. Thiệu also said it was time to plan for Aunt Mỹ's marriage.

Despite the woman's objections, Aunt Mỹ left her. She took turns living between her two older sisters, Tiệu and Tạo, and helped harvest crops. Her chores also included traveling miles on foot to distant farms to purchase sweet potatoes and cassava at low prices. She would then resell these items at the local market for a measly profit. Additionally, she had to mill paddy rice to provide for the family.

During this period, rice was expensive, scarce, and controlled by local authorities. Only families registered in the *hộ khẩu* (household registration books) were entitled to buy a small rice allowance. As Aunt Mỹ's name wasn't registered anywhere, she couldn't access this allowance and had to share the meager portions allotted to her sisters' families. Aunt Mỹ eventually married her husband, Trần Ngọc Cung, and had children. However, Aunt Mỹ's life did not improve after marriage, and she continued to grapple with poverty and hunger for decades.

Aunt Mièu

After Aunt Mỹ left the market with the woman who owned the textile shop, Aunt Mièu continued to beg for food on the street alongside her grandmother. When the seven year old girl was lucky to find bits of discarded food, she would share it with her grandma.

One day, a woman approached her grandmother and asked if Aunt Mièu could live with her to be a helper. Hoping for a better life for little Mièu, her grandma agreed, and Aunt Mièu went to live with the woman, who resided several miles away. That was the last time Aunt Mièu saw her grandma, who soon passed away from hunger, with no one to care for her.

Once settled with the woman, Aunt Mièu was tasked with tending to water buffaloes in the field. At such a young age, she didn't know how to manage the buffaloes, and she couldn't even distinguish which buffalo belonged to the family.

That evening, when Aunt Mièu returned home without the buffaloes, the woman grew angry and threatened to starve her if she didn't perform her duties the next day.

The following morning, Aunt Mièu headed toward a bridge leading to a neighboring village, intending to leave and abandon her task. However, someone saw that she was trying to escape, and this person decided to intervene. To punish her and to teach her a lesson, he held her by her feet and repeatedly dipped her head into the river! He only stopped when Aunt Mièu cried, pleaded, and promised to stay and work.

Yet, as night fell, Aunt Miều managed to escape again. Crossing the bridge, though unsure of her direction, she determined to find her way to her home village.

She walked for a full day, exhausted, hungry, and thirsty under the boiling sun. She told herself that if she kept putting one foot in front of the other, soon she would be home.

Miraculously, Aunt Miều found her way back to her oldest sister, Aunt Thiệu. She believed her late parents had protected her. Although Aunt Thiệu was happy to see her younger sister safe, she lacked the means to support Aunt Miều. Consequently, Aunt Miều continued to beg for food at the market.

Soon afterward, a man named Quý approached Aunt Miều. His wife had experienced repeated miscarriages, prompting him to adopt an orphan in hopes of receiving a blessing from God — the gift of a son.

When Mr. Quý brought Aunt Miều to his home, the entire village gathered, almost treating it like a spectacle. Aunt Miều became a helper of the family, and when Mr. Quý's wife eventually gave birth to a son, the baby grew fondly attached to Aunt Miều, as she had cared for him from his birth.

Uncle Thuỵ

After Aunts Miều and Mỹ found themselves families to work for in exchange for a place to stay, Uncle Thuỵ continued to wander around the market, begging for discarded food or scouring the landfill in search of something to eat. He was ten years old.

A family asked Thuỵ to help them with chores in trade for a place to stay and daily food. Thuỵ gladly accepted the offer. He did not mind the arduous labor as long as he did not have to beg for food in the street. His job was to tend the buffaloes and help in the field, tilling, seeding, weeding, and harvesting. He worked there until Dad intervened, creating a new life for Thuỵ and their sister Miều.

Dad Returned

Dad was imprisoned for 18 months in Hỏa-Lò prison for attempting to escape to South Vietnam. Upon his release in 1958, he headed straight home and discovered that his younger siblings had been scattered.

Knowing that he could never be allowed to live under the

communist government as "a descendent of a landowner family," Dad planned to escape to South Vietnam again. But first, Dad and his cousin Khâm decided to find the younger siblings and ensure their well-being.

First, Dad had to find a place for Uncle Thụy. He knew a priest who lived in Xã Đoài village, so he took the 13-year-old Thụy there and asked Father Năng to take him in. The compassionate priest adopted Uncle Thụy.

Since Father Năng was a poor priest who had to work hard in the field to survive, Uncle Thụy also had to labor. Fortunately, during the years he lived with Father Năng, Uncle Thụy was able to go to school and often returned to his hometown to visit his older sisters.

Dad and Khâm then found Mr. Nguỵ, who appeared to be caring and genuinely devoted to Uncle Lĩnh as his own child. Seeing that, Dad decided it was a good idea that Uncle Lĩnh stay where he was. Mr. Nguỵ welcomed Dad and Khâm to stay overnight before leaving to find Aunt Miều.

After four years of separation, Aunt Miều was now ten years old, and it was hard for Dad to recognize her. However, the birthmark on her face confirmed her identity. Tears and emotions flowed as they reunited. Aunt Miều was overjoyed to see Dad again.

When asked whether she wished to stay with Mr. Quý's family or return home with Aunt Thiệu, she chose to come home. The Quý family was sad to see her go. Dad explained to Aunt Miều that despite the seemingly kind treatment she received as a helper in the Quý household, he wanted her to return home so that she could have the opportunity to attend school.

Dad brought Aunt Miều back to Aunt Thiệu and enrolled her in first grade. Then, a distant relative named Phòng, a midwife and widow, kindly offered to take Aunt Miều in.

Aunt Mìều lived with Mrs. Phòng for several years and managed to complete sixth grade. However, when Aunt Mìều turned 13, Mrs. Phòng remarried, and Aunt Mìều again had to fend for herself, doing whatever she could to survive.

During the day, she scoured the fields for leftover crops discarded by harvesters to trade for food at the market. She also collected discarded rice from the paddy storage, carefully sifting through the grains to separate the hulls from the usable rice kernels. Sometimes, she ventured into the forest to collect wood, selling it at the market or trading it for sustenance. Despite her arduous efforts to survive, she continued to study at night.

When Mìều was 19 years old, a kind relative in the village gave her an allowance for a large bush of bamboo trees. Aunt Mìều chopped some bamboo to construct a small hut at the base of the bamboo trees and made a home there.

Later, she met her husband, Nguyễn Xuân Nam, who was skilled in bicycle repair. Like her sister Mỹ, she continued to endure a hard life of demanding labor for decades.

Two brothers reunite

After Uncle Thuy turned 16, he left Father Năng's diocese. He sought laboring jobs so he could support himself. He helped farmers in their fields and worked at the market to earn meager money.

In his mid-20s, Uncle Thuy searched for and found his younger brother, Lĩnh. Together, the two brothers worked on odd jobs for a living. They cut wood in the forest to sell to local lumber businesses and carried pottery for miles from the village's pottery plants to the market for resale. They also helped the farmers in the fields in exchange for food.

By the time Uncle Thuy reached his early 30s, he had fallen in love with Aunt Lệ, a beautiful seventeen-year-old girl. As anticipated, Aunt Lệ's family opposed their relationship. The biggest reason was that Aunt Lệ's family also had been suffering severe political punishment from the government;

as a result, they did not want Aunt Lệ to make her life worse by marrying a son of a condemned landowner. Moreover, Uncle Thuỵ was 14 years older than her and still empty-handed.

However, overcoming numerous objections from Aunt Lệ's family, Uncle Thuỵ and Aunt Lệ chose to marry and build a life together. Aunt Lệ told her family that she had confidence in Uncle Thuỵ's resilience and ability to endure and conquer life's challenges, no matter how difficult.

Despite the hardships of their daily lives, filled with demanding labor to make ends meet, they found happiness in each other's company.

Chapter 7: The Escape Plan

Looking for their brother

Back to the time when Uncles Thuỵ and Lĩnh visited us in Tà Keo, they shared with Dad about their lives of extreme poverty in North Vietnam.

Fortunately, through hard work and the spiritual protection of their late parents, they overcame tragedy, grew up, and built their own families. Most importantly, they stayed close to one another, continuing to remind each other of the horrific tragedy their parents endured under the communist authorities. Despite spending years at the bottom of society, they took pride in their honorable parents, who came from an upper-class background. Above all, they remembered that their parents would have wanted them to love and support each other.

Because of Vietnam's civil war, they did not have any contact with Dad for decades after Dad escaped to South Vietnam. Under a rare fortunate chance in 1959, Dad sent them the news that he had arrived in Hue. They were happy that Dad was alive and dreamt that one day, Dad could come back to visit them all. In 1975, as soon as the Vietnam War ended, Uncles Thuỵ and Lĩnh headed south to look for Dad.

Although Vietnam was expected to become a unified country in April 1975, and the border between North and South Vietnam was removed, travel between the two regions remained heavily restricted for a long time. If individuals from North Vietnam were caught attempting to cross to the South, they faced imprisonment.

My uncles had to navigate past the vigilant military who constantly monitored the bridge spanning the Hiền Lương River, which marked the separation point between North and South Vietnam. Under cover of darkness and right under the noses of armed guards, they edged along

the bottom side of the bridge under the guards, endangering their lives as they dangled over the churning river below.

They journeyed at night and hid during the day, evading watch-posts. Once, while hiding in the bushes beside the highway at night, they encountered foxes gazing at them in the darkness with gleaming eyes.

For weeks, they moved southward by jumping trains, hiding in the backs of rice trucks, and hitchhiking on wagons. They avoided the main road as much as possible, and fortunately, they found that many South Vietnamese sympathized with them and helped them avoid the authorities.

It took them weeks to get to Sài Gòn with the bit of money that was their life savings. The suspenseful details of this trip could fill up another book!

Living with the uncles

Uncles Thuỵ and Lĩnh stayed with us for a month. Throughout their visit, they assisted Dad with fieldwork. They excavated canals to irrigate the fields. They repurposed the soil from the excavation to construct elevated banks alongside the canals, where they cultivated banana and coconut trees—plants that thrive and yield fruits quickly in Vietnam. The field was saturated with water heavily tainted by iron oxides, so they were compelled to cultivate sweet potatoes instead of rice, given the contamination in the water.

One day, my brother Lĩnh (yes, sharing the name with Uncle Lĩnh) and my cousin Tín, both five years old, were playing in the kitchen near the stove. My other brother, Yên, and cousin Toàn, who were three years old, were nearby. Aunt Hoài, engrossed in preparing a meal for our extended family, was unaware that the boys were toying with fire, using the hay she used to cook.

In seconds, the fire caught onto one side of the kitchen and rapidly spread out, threatening to burn down the entire house, which was constructed primarily with dry hay.

Aunt Hoài and the little ones hurried out of the kitchen, their cries for help echoing across the house.

Immediately, Mom instructed my brother Tuyến to carry infant baby Nhon, who was asleep in my parents' bed beside the kitchen. Simultaneously, Mom hurriedly moved gasoline cans stored beneath the bed, dragging them as far away from the fire as possible.

Meanwhile, uncles Lĩnh, Thuỵ, Huệ, Hạnh, Hậu, and Dad were tending to the nearby field in preparation for planting crops.

Upon hearing the distressed cries, Uncle Lĩnh instinctively sprinted toward the kitchen. Snatching the straw mat from Mom's bed, he jumped on the roof and quickly used it to beat at the advancing flames. The fire was extinguished in just a few minutes, and Uncle Lĩnh emerged as the hero! Without his swift action, we would have faced the devastating loss of everything to the flames.

Uncles Thuỵ and Lĩnh stayed with us for a month before returning to their hometown. We were all sad to see them go.

Dad asked them to bring their families to live with us because, in comparison, life was easier in the South than in the North. However, Uncle Lĩnh decided to stay put because he already had a family with two young children. He also wanted to stay in his hometown to care for the family ancestors' shrines.

On the other hand, Uncle Thuỵ soon came back with his wife, Aunt Lệ. They built a little straw hut near our house. Not long later, they had two cute little girls, Ri and Ngọc. I often heard my uncle and aunt teach them to sing sweet, funny folk songs from their hometown. They would sing to us whenever we requested—such beautiful memories.

Uncle Thuỵ and Lệ worked very hard in their field and were able to stock a storage room with rice. Chickens, ducks, and pigs roamed their yard.

The Escape Plan

One night, I overheard Dad and Uncle Thuy talking by our house.

Dad said, "We must learn to navigate the sea from the local fishermen and catch fish along the coast. Then, when we know our ways well at sea, we take the family and cross the ocean to Thailand. There are only a few weeks in March when the sea is calm, and that would be the best time for us to escape."

The plan began to form. Dad hired the locals to build a boat.

Meanwhile, Dad, Uncle Thuy, and Uncle Huệ began learning fishing techniques from the locals. Occasionally, my brother Tuyến joined them. The goal was to convince the local authorities that they were genuine fishermen. After the boat was built, Dad and his crew engaged in regular fishing expeditions. The local coastguard became familiar with Dad's crew, and they no longer halted his boat for paperwork checks as it passed them on its way to the ocean.

In this escape plan, Mom was assigned a specific role. She traveled to Sài Gòn to recruit "customers"—friends and relatives interested in joining the escape. These individuals contributed money to pay for the boat's construction and the associated paperwork fees (which involved bribing the local authorities).

Our home began receiving more visitors from the city who were interested in the plan. At night, the adults huddled around the dinner table illuminated by an oil lamp to have secretive discussions.

For us children, it meant having more playmates from the city now and then. We proudly showed these city kids, pale and timid in the field, how to navigate rural life. It was truly satisfying!

It took Dad several years to become a proficient fisherman. Dad, Uncle Huệ, and the crew ventured out to sea regularly, sometimes spending days away. I missed Dad during those times. We fretted when storms brewed and fervently prayed for the crew's safety. Often, I would stay up, waiting for the sound of Dad's boat approaching the shore.

Upon its return, the boat would be laden with various fish species, some of which I had never seen before. Dad sold the catch to a fishing company, reserving only a small portion for our family's consumption.

My siblings and I relished exploring the slimy and pungent heaps, curiously examining unfamiliar fish. The excitement peaked when we discovered little seahorses resembling creatures from fairy tales, peculiar-looking sea stars, semi-transparent puffer fish that exposed their organs through their skin, and notably the menacing stingrays with dark skin and tails adorned with sharp blades.

During the crew's breaks and when they weren't out at sea, Uncle Huệ stayed on the boat as a guard. As far back as I can recall, Uncle Huệ was a constant presence with my family, steadfastly by Dad's side.

He possessed a gentle disposition, was loyal, and had a penchant for dreaming, unfazed by solitude. He was often spotted savoring dark coffee, smoking his Laos pipe, and composing music. As he slept on the boat, his melodies seemed to harmonize with the rhythmic rocking of the waves and their gentle lapping against the hull. Most of his compositions were love songs dedicated to an enchanting woman who lived in a distant place.

Between fishing trips, Dad tended to the fields and made repairs around the farm and at the house. At night, my siblings and I eagerly piled onto my parents' bed to be near him. We took turns sleeping in their bed; it was a cherished part of the day.

By then, Dad's complexion had darkened, and he appeared to be more toned and muscular. He could converse in the local dialect when necessary. To the locals, he had become one of their own—an adept farmer and fisherman. Most importantly, he had become well-acquainted with the coastline.

I remained awestruck by Dad's resilience and capacity to adapt. Initially, he had to suppress his remarkable individuality to assume a role he was not accustomed to—a farmer with limited reading and writing skills. Subsequently, he shouldered the responsibility for everyone's safety, toiling ceaselessly to secure a better life for us.

Above all, I was amazed by his unwavering faith and inner strength. Dad never surrendered. He believed that with God on his side, he would extricate us from our dire circumstances and guide us to a brighter future, free from hiding and full of opportunities.

In 1978, armed with a newly constructed boat, Dad was prepared to embark on the ocean-crossing plan.

After meticulously plotting our escape for years, Dad put his plan into action. Our cover story was that Dad and Uncle Huệ were going fishing, but they would rendezvous with the rest of our family and others who paid to join our escape. They would navigate the boat down the river toward the sea, and at night, when the coast would be clear of coastguards, the rest of the family would ride in smaller boats to meet up with Dad at a predetermined location.

However, things unfolded differently than planned. After three days of Dad "fishing" in the same spot along the coast, the coastguards from Trà Vinh City searched his boat. They discovered piles of books and delicate porcelain tableware Mom had hidden in a compartment below deck. Who would pack books when trying to escape? Only Mom would have such a silly idea!

Because Vietnamese fishermen were unlikely to read literature or dine with fine porcelain while catching fish, these items made it clear that Dad and his crew were not legitimate fishermen. As a result, Dad and Uncle Huệ were arrested for plotting an escape.

Fortunately, Mom had the wisdom to bribe the officers and build friendly relationships with people at the station. Instead of being sent to prison for treason, as was typical for escapees, the officers kept Dad and Uncle Huệ at the security station. Mom frequently visited, bringing gifts and befriending the guards. Though Dad and Uncle Huệ had to assist with daily tasks, they were allowed to eat and sleep alongside the officers. They even permitted Mom to stay overnight in the same bed as Dad!

The officers viewed Dad and Uncle Huệ as uneducated fishermen, so their case was deemed unimportant. After a year, Dad and Uncle Huệ were released without any lasting consequences.

As soon as Dad returned home, with the little money left from selling the rest of the gold, he started planning another escape.

This time, Dad determined there would be no room for failure. If we failed, we would be empty-handed, and our family would be doomed to a life of poverty forever.

Chapter 8:
The Journey to a New Land

(Like Chapter 1, this chapter is written from Dad's perspective, using the information from recordings of his conversations, his memoir, and countless times he shared stories with family and friends.)

Crossing the ocean

March 8, 1980
We spent another two years carefully planning the last escape. This time, I had to ensure we weren't arrested again. If they caught us now, we'd be empty-handed and might end up begging on the street. I could never let that happen to my family!

Like last time, our plan were to go to the ocean and pretended to fish while Huệ, Tuyến, and two customers' sons acted as my crew. My wife and her other brothers were to guide everyone to meet us off the coast at our designated meeting spot. From there, we would journey across the border of Vietnam and escaped to Thailand.

On a fine day in February 1980, when the sea water was supposed to be calm and best for a voyage across the ocean, we ran our fishing boat south to Phú Quốc Island and anchored off the coast. The coastguard closely observed us "fishing," ensuring we weren't picking up any "customers." This act had become quite popular, as many others had attempted it. As a result, the coastguard was aware of this activity and did its best to prevent it. Thankfully, the coastguard only watched us from a distance and didn't approach us with questions. We were safe! We fished and waited until night fell.

"Something is wrong. It's been three days, but they are still not here."

"By tonight, even if we don't see them, we have to leave."

Tuyến bowed his head. He looked sad. I tried to comfort him, "I don't want to leave without them, but we can't stay here too long, son. If we do, we'll be arrested and left empty-handed, begging on the street."

When the sun rose, I knew I couldn't wait any longer. Staying in one place near the coastline and circling might make the coastal police suspicious, so that night, we set off into the deep sea. We did not know if we would ever see our loved ones again, and we were not even sure we could reach the other side of the ocean alive.

With heavy hearts, we headed toward Thailand.

RẠCH GIÁ

THAILAND
Songkhla

The ocean water was initially clear and blue, but as we traveled farther, it grew dark, almost black, hinting at its great depth. Fear and sadness washed over us every time we looked at it; the brackish water carried an overwhelming sense of depression. I had heard stories of people who jumped into the sea, their minds gripped by terror. We reminded each other not to look down to avoid that dreadful feeling.

We continued for two nights and two days without incident. At this point, we had already entered international waters.

We once encountered a magnificent vessel with numerous people on board. It could have been a Western cruise ship or a private yacht. They simply looked at us as we passed by.

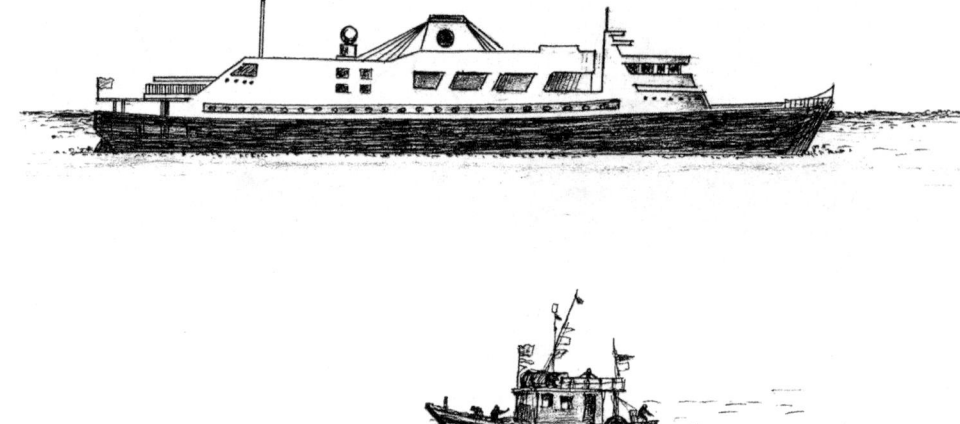

Later that evening, we spotted another large boat. At first, we thought it was just another peaceful vessel, so we waved to them. Little did we know it was a Thai fishing boat. Compared to our small craft, we looked like a skinny stray dog standing beside a giant lion. We soon discovered this "lion" was a predator! They abruptly cut in front of our boat. The men were aggressive and carried sharp machetes and swords. One mean-looking man shouted something to his peers.

The Thai fishermen jumped onto our boat. While some kept us at sword-point, others tossed things around, searching for valuables. They screamed at us as they went through our boat.

Like the coastal police, these Thai fishermen knew about the Vietnamese "boat escapers." They took advantage of the situation, intercepting boats full of people, robbing them, and leaving them with nothing. Much later, I heard countless horrifying stories of how these pirates sought money and raped women, girls, and boys. Many victims were taken to Thailand to be sold into prostitution.

After the pirates left, our boat was in a terrible state. These monstrous men had emptied every container of food. When they opened the rice can, a large amount of rice spilled onto the floor and got into the water pump engine, making it jammed. And worse, their boat was so big that it created waves that flooded our boat as it passed. Without a functioning water pump, we were in danger of sinking. We struggled to remove the water from the boat using any containers we could find. By the time we could empty most of the water, we were utterly exhausted.

After the incident, I realized that it was God's plan for my wife, daughters, and the other women in our group not to make it onto our boat. I couldn't bear the thought of those awful and violent individuals laying hands on my loved ones.

Throughout that evening, we encountered at least a dozen more similar robberies. Like the first pirates, these men would approach us, intimidate us with their weapons, and create chaos. However, since they didn't find anything of value, they would eventually leave. On one occasion, a pirate picked up my Latin Bible while looking around; he then glanced at me and walked away with it. Looking back, I find it amusing—a literate pirate?

At last, the robberies ended, and we were left alone for the night.

Sailing into Thailand

We continue to drive the boat forward. But there was a problem.

"The pirates took my compass!" I said.
"What will you do?" Huệ asked.
"I will try to use the stars as our guide," I replied.

While controlling the boat, I showed my son Tuyến how to use the North Star to find directions. I learned this skill while serving in the South Vietnamese Army Reserve.

Then, in the darkness, one of the boys spotted a sliver of land on the horizon—Thailand!

While I steered the boat toward it, Huệ and the others worked tirelessly to bail out the water leaking into the lower deck.

After a while, we decided to drop the anchor and take a break. Exhausted from the dreadful events of the previous evening and our efforts to keep the boat afloat all night, we all fell asleep.

When we woke up, the sun was high in the sky.

I'm hungry. Do we have anything to eat, Uncle?

They spilled all the food! We have nothing left!

Trying to ignore our hunger, we kept steering the boat toward the land until clusters of beautiful purple flowers floated toward us. Years of working on the water had taught us that the roots of those flowers could tangle in the propeller and stop our engine. Still, we felt a spark of excitement—they signaled we were leaving the ocean and entering the rivers.

We moved further inland. At first, we saw people along the shore working on their boats and doing various tasks. Then, we came across bustling markets along the river, filled with crowds. When people saw us, they seemed friendly and kind.

We docked our boat at the riverbank near what looked like a small elementary school. Huệ jumped ashore to seek help while we stayed in the boat.

Using his limited French and gestures, he communicated with some teachers, who gave him directions and a small amount of money to take a bus to the nearest police station. After a long time, Huệ returned, accompanied by a few Thai policemen. We left our boat and followed them ashore to their headquarters, where they offered us food, water, and a resting bench.

Around 40 or 50 Vietnamese people were already there. It seemed like we had arrived at the right place; these people were familiar with Vietnamese boat refugees. They allowed us to stay at the station for a few days. Huệ kept himself occupied by assisting the staff with translation. Some doctors were sent to provide medical care for the Vietnamese refugees. They spoke French, and Huệ was fluent, so he was glad to help.

Once enough people filled two buses, we were transferred to the Songkhla refugee camp in southern Thailand. The donor governments primarily funded these refugee camps through the United Nations High Commissioner for Refugees (UNHCR). We were assigned a place to stay and provided with daily meals and essential supplies. They even provided us with stamps to communicate with our families back home.

As soon as I settled, I wrote two letters—one to my wife in Vietnam and another to Father Cao Văn Luận, who lived in Belgium. It took a couple of months for my letter to reach my wife, as was typical then.

However, the letter I wrote to Father Luận arrived more quickly. He sent a telegram to my wife, which was a faster method despite being more expensive. My wife, who had been deeply distressed and had not heard of her husband and son for weeks, could finally find some hope.

While living in the camp, we occasionally heard announcements welcoming new refugees over the loudspeakers. We always eagerly listened to see if we recognized any of the names. After a few months at the refugee camp, Father Cao Văn Luận found a church that sponsored our relocation to Northern California. We were to board a plane to America.

On the day we were to leave for California, we heard the names of my younger brother Thụy, his wife, Lệ, and their two daughters in the welcoming announcement. Since we were about to board the bus to the airport, we couldn't meet them. However, when we reunited much later in America, Thụy shared his story of crossing the sea.

Story from Thuỵ: Another escape from pirates

After I left Rạch Giá, Thuỵ decided to take his family across the ocean in his old boat. Despite the boat's small size and lack of seaworthiness, they were willing to take their chances, even though Lệ was very pregnant.

At one point, their engine stopped working. They were adrift for several days with dwindling food and water supplies. When the pirates came near, they were surprised to see such a fragile boat in the vast ocean, carrying a family with a pregnant woman and two young children.

One of the pirates remarked, "It's a bad omen to encounter a pregnancy at sea," and they quickly left.

Other pirates approached them but also hurriedly departed.

The last Thai fishing boat they encountered took pity on them. They provided them with water and food and even helped tow their damaged boat to the shore. As soon as they reached land, Thụy's boat completely fell apart! His wife was immediately taken to the hospital, where she gave birth to their third daughter, Mai.

Once they joined us in California, Thụy and his family worked diligently, establishing a gardening business and creating a prosperous life for themselves. They have three more children. All of their children attended school and adapted well to life in America.

Arriving in California

My son, Huệ, and I arrived in San Jose, California, in the summer of 1980. We began settling down with the assistance of a local church. They provided us with clothing, helped Huệ and me secure jobs at a gas station, and guided my son Tuyến through enrolling in a nearby middle school.

Tuyến was 15 years old at the time. He adapted well to the new culture, benefiting from his young age. He completed high school and pursued a college education, initially studying engineering but transitioning to an art university to become an art director in advertising design.

Huệ obtained an Associate degree from a city college and worked as a teaching assistant before eventually joining a computer company.

I decided to further my education by pursuing a Bachelor's degree in engineering and a Master's in computer science. My goal was to obtain a good job that would allow me to bring my family to live with me.

While in school, I used my strong math skills to work as a tutor on campus. At the same time, I continued my job at the gas station to cover food and rent and to send $50 to my wife in Vietnam every month.

Stories from home

My wife and I continued to exchange letters. It took approximately two weeks for our letters to reach each other. She explained in one of her letters why their boat couldn't meet us at the shore as planned.

On the scheduled meeting day, my wife, our children, and the other passengers hid beneath the boat's roof at sunset. Her brothers Bê-Em and Hậu dressed as local fishermen heading to the market to disguise their boat and avoid detection. They strategically piled fishnets on the deck to resemble a fishing boat. They drove the boat past the security checkpoints without arousing suspicion from the coastguard.

When they reached the area where the river met the ocean, our meeting place, they searched for my fishing boat. In a moment of distraction, one of my wife's brothers inadvertently caused a glare when he pulled out the binoculars to scan the horizon. The setting sun reflected off the binoculars, catching the coastguard's attention at a distance.

Immediately, the guards boarded a speedboat and began their approach. Sensing the danger, Hậu swiftly steered the boat toward the dense mangrove palm forest lining the coast. Hiding beneath the lower deck, everyone was terrified to hear gunshots.

Miraculously, the coastguard's bullets narrowly missed the boat as Hậu skillfully zigzagged through the rough waves. The battering waves partially submerged the passengers hidden at the bottom of the boat.

The frightened children felt unwell from the turbulent ride. They cried, and some vomited. My wife did her best to comfort the sick children while simultaneously bailing out water to prevent the boat from sinking.

Fortunately, the sun had set entirely. Hậu turned off the engine in the darkness, allowing the boat to glide into the thick shade of the mangrove palm forest.

The coastguard halted their pursuit. They refrained from entering the forest, likely assuming that my wife's brothers were Khmer Rouge spies, possibly armed for self-defense. Our town was near the Cambodian border, and at that time, the remnants of Pol Pot's forces still hid in the jungle. After their defeat by the Vietnamese army, they continued guerrilla warfare along the border. Seeing only two men dressed in black, the coastguard acted cautiously. After a while, they chose not to approach our hiding place and left.

When they were sure the guards had left, still under the protection of the darkness provided by the mangrove palm forest at night, Hậu quietly moved the boat closer to the shore, where the water was shallow enough for people to walk. My wife told the passengers that the escape plan had failed. She instructed all the adult passengers to jump off the boat and find their way to leave town, returning to the city where they came from. Only Hậu and Bê-Em remained in the boat with my wife and children.

Before the sky grew brighter at dawn, Hậu silently steered the boat out of the forest and guided it toward the river. The market was bustling with activity, and as they passed the security checkpoints, their boat blended in with the others. With my wife and children casually sitting on the deck, they appeared like an ordinary family returning home after a trip to the market.

My family felt immense sadness as she realized they missed the opportunity to meet us. They feared they might never see me, Tuyến, and Huệ again. Weeks passed without any news about me, our son, or her brother. The Vietnamese New Year arrived, but there was no cause or money to celebrate. Sitting in an empty hut devoid of food, flowers, and cheerful greetings from relatives, my wife and the children believed we might be lost at the bottom of the ocean.

After I contacted Father Cao Văn Luận, he sent a telegram to my wife's sister Hoà, who lived in Sai-Gon. Since the place where we lived on the farm did not have an address, that was the only address to which we could send the news. One of my wife's sisters, Mộng-Huyền, took a bus to bring the news to my wife and the children. It took her all day to get there.

My wife immediately shook off her depressive mood and devised a new plan. She contacted people she knew, gathering funds to build another boat, hoping to cross the ocean to Thailand. Those who contributed money would join the escape when the time came.

HUNGQ . HUEJ. BU. DEWNS NOIW BINHQ AN

Telegram informed the safe arrival

The plan would take three years. During that time, distressing news about Vietnamese boat people targeted by pirates became more frequent. Women and children got raped and trafficked to prostitution while men lost their lives. I couldn't bear the thought of my wife and children embarking on such an arduous journey and falling into the hands of those monsters.

I urged my wife to abandon the plan. Instead, I asked her to take the children to Sài Gòn, where they could receive a better education, learn English, and prepare for their future in America. We assured the individuals who had contributed money to the escape plan that I would repay the debt, which I later did. I then promptly began the paperwork to sponsor my family's immigration to America.

Little did I know that it would take nearly ten years to see my family again.

(End of Dad's narration)

Chapter 9: Staying Behind

The "Rau Ngổ" Alley

After Dad left, we faced a life of extreme poverty.

While Mom and Grandma stayed on the farm with my youngest siblings, Yên and Mi-Nhon, Mom decided the older kids had to move to the nearby town so that we could attend school.

Aunt Hoà and her five children, my sister Nu, my brother Lĩnh, and I stayed in a humble hut that had been initially a pig pen. Sitting at the end of a muddy alley, clustered with run-down shacks on both sides, this was a place we could afford due to the cheap rent. Aunt Hoà's husband and his brother, Uncle Tâm and Uncle Sơn, worked quickly to build a few bamboo beds and a table, making the place somewhat livable.

To create an extra room for us to do homework during the day, they constructed another bamboo table at the front of the hut. Adjacent to the hut stood a massive gravestone. Initially, sitting near it made us uneasy, but with time, we all became accustomed to its presence. I was 13 years old and in eighth grade at the time. I remember a boy from my class once stopping by to greet me. As I casually worked on my homework at the front table, feeling flattered that

I had caught his attention, he stood there, gazing at the gravestone, appearing uncomfortable, and eventually left.

Next to the hut was a tiny pond the whole neighborhood used for washing. Unfortunately, the water was so contaminated that it appeared yellow and thick, resembling orange juice. Despite its condition, we had no choice but to use that water to clean dishes, clothes, and ourselves.

An old military helmet had been repurposed as a makeshift pail, which everyone in the neighborhood shared to scoop water from the pond. People would wash themselves, dishes, and clothes there, and the dirty water would flow back into the same pond!

We relied on rainwater collected in ceramic barrels throughout the year for cooking. During dry spells, we bought clean water from neighbors fortunate to have running water from faucets. Clean water was considered precious and rare in those times. Nearby was a bigger pond where people cultivated rau ngổ (a rice paddy herb), which led to the neighborhood being called Rau Ngổ Alley. The pond also served as a place to raise catfish for sale in markets.

People built a small stilted box in a corner of the pond using palm leaves and bamboo. This was our neighborhood's outhouse. Using it could be pretty embarrassing since everyone could see your head sticking out of the box. Furthermore, the catfish would rush over to eat the droppings whenever someone used the outhouse, creating quite a scene!

The roof of our hut was made of palm leaves. When it rained, water dripped through the thatched roof and spilled down on us. We placed a plastic tarp over our mosquito net on the bed to stay dry at night. During heavy rains and floods, water from the outside ponds would seep into our hut, carrying unpleasant things from the ponds.

At night, several of us would share a bed. Since we usually didn't have electricity, we had to study under the dim light of a small oil lamp. My sister Nu, my cousin Ty, and I took turns cooking in a tiny clay wood-fueled oven. We had to prepare meals on the ground. Our typical dishes were cooked rice with stir-fried vegetables and small bits of minced pork.

On weekends, I would often try to return to the farm. Compared to the city hut, our place on the farm offered a wonderful escape with fresh air and plenty of space. Eventually, Yên also came to the city for school, leaving my youngest sister, Mi-Nhon, with Mom and Grandma.

The poor little girl had no one to play with, so she was always excited when I visited. We would make paper dolls and play house together, using chopped leaves and flowers as make-believe food. It was difficult when I had to leave her. Standing by the riverbank with tears in her eyes, my sister tried not to cry as she watched the leaf boat carry me further away from her.

We lived in Rau Ngổ Alley for two years. One day, Mom told us, "Dad wrote that I should stop planning for the escape. Instead, we need to move to Sài-Gòn, where you children can attend better schools and study English to prepare for eventually living in America." Of course, we were all happy to leave that dumpster behind!

However, the hard part was saying goodbye to our dog, Xay-nai, who was with us for eight years.

Saying goodbye to Xay-Nai

Xay-Nai had been with our family through good times and bad. He hunted snakes and mice with us, swam in the river, ran in the fields, and stayed by our side even when we had little to eat.

We didn't know where to stay next, and finding shelter depended on the kindness of friends and relatives. Finding a place for our big family, let alone a giant dog, was already challenging.

With heavy hearts, we climbed into a canoe and paddled away, leaving Xay-nai behind.

At first, Xay-Nai stood on the riverbank, looking at us worriedly.

Then, he jumped into the
river and swam after our canoe
for a long time.

When he was tired from
swimming, he paddled back to
the shore and ran along the riverbank until the small river joined
a larger one, and he could no longer follow us.

Finally, he just stood there at the edge
of the river, howling for us.

Much later, Mom made a short trip back to our old farm. She went to our hut and found it gone. The local people must have taken it apart for firewood, leaving only the bare dirt floor.

Mom asked the neighbors about Xay-Nai. They said that after we left, he wandered around the neighborhood daily. The neighbors fed him some discarded food, and sometimes, they saw him catching mice or snakes in the fields.

Every night, he returned to the bare land where our hut used to be and fell asleep. One night, he slept but never woke up. The neighbor buried him on the edge of that land, by the river that took us away from him. I cried when I heard this story. I wondered if his spirit was still waiting for us at the end of that river. Would he understand that we didn't mean to desert him? That we had no choice but to leave him behind, alone? Would dogs go to a place in the afterlife to reunite with their owners?

Would he ever forgive us?

Chapter 10: Nomadic Life

Getting Used to City Life, 1982

We had been "hiding" in Rạch Giá for over seven years. When we left Rạch Giá, I was 14 years old and had just finished eighth grade. My sister Nu was 16, my brother Lĩnh was 11, my brother Yên was 9, and my youngest sister Minhon was 6.

Dad had written to Mom about the change of plan for us; he wanted us to stop the scheme to escape out of the country by boat. Instead, he told us we should move to Sài-Gòn, where we would go to school, learn English, and prepare for life in America.

In the meantime, Dad was in America, going to school and working two jobs. As a new refugee in America, Dad struggled to make ends meet. He could only send us $50 US monthly to cover our living expenses. With little money and no place to call home, we relied on the kindness of others to get by. We also pitched in by caring for one another, as we always had.

Since Dad left, Mom has been brave and strong, caring for the five of us alone. She was a fighter. She never showed any signs of fear or discouragement. Despite life's challenges and our uncertain future, my siblings and I always felt secure because we knew Mom would find solutions, no matter how difficult the situation.

We stood on the brink of yet another chapter in our lives, living day by day, waiting to reunite with Dad and my oldest brother Tuyến in America. Little did we know that it would take another grueling seven years before that moment would come.

Mom took us to a bus station to reach Sài Gòn, the same station we had come to eight years ago when we arrived in Rạch-Giá seeking refuge from the new government. After April 1975, the city's name was changed from Sài Gòn to Hồ Chí Minh city. But like many people from South Vietnam, we would always reminiscently call it by its original name, Sài Gòn.

The bus reminded me of the last time we traveled seven years ago with Dad, except this bus was much older and smellier. More bags were in the middle aisle, and more animals were under the seats. The bags were filled with rice, potatoes, and other produce that people would resell in Sài-Gòn. The heat and odors made us feel choked.

To add to the smells of sweat and urine in the crowded bus, Yên started to vomit. Luckily, Mom was sitting near him and acted quickly. She was holding a bag containing the rice bars we had made earlier for the trip. She dumped the food onto my lap and reached to catch Yên's barf. Nu pulled a handkerchief out of her pocket so Mom could wipe Yên's face.

The stench of the vomit made me feel like I was about to throw up. I clenched my teeth hard and tried to turn toward the windows for some air. Gladly, the bus started moving. The cool breeze made me feel better. The rumbling of the vehicle was calming. I eventually dozed off.

When we arrived at Sài Gòn, it was dusk. When we stepped off the bus, men rushed to the passengers, surrounding us like birds trying to eat from the same pile of seeds. They were tricycle drivers trying to get customers. After bargaining back and forth, Mom settled on two older men who agreed to take us for a price less than the other men asked.

Three of us shared one tricycle. We piled our bags on the tricycles and sat on one another to fit on the carriage. The poor men, who were petite and skinny, were stronger than I thought. They started to step on the paddles, and the tricycle rolled slowly but eventually faster on the street.

The streets were sometimes steep, so the men jumped off their seats and pushed the carriage on foot. We felt terrible for them, and Mom asked our drivers if they wanted us to get down. However, they insisted that we stay put.

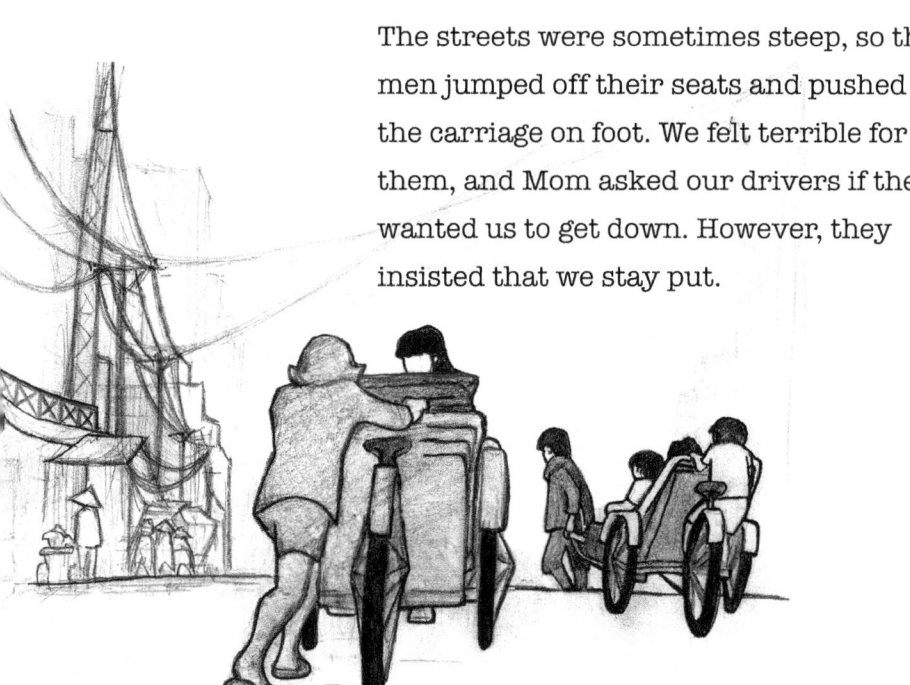

When we rode down the street, my siblings and I couldn't help but look around to take in the scenery. After years of living in quiet rural places, Sài Gòn seemed busy and big. Compared to the little town of Rạch Giá, where we had just come from, the stores here were bigger, the lights were brighter, and the streets looked much neater. Food vendors lined the road with hot pots steaming, sending off delicious aromas. The sidewalks were crowded with pedestrians, and I had never seen so many bicycles!

We finally arrived at a house in a tree-shaded alley with thick branches overhead. Beyond the gate, guarded by towering trees, stood a quaint brick house with a tiled roof and a front yard full of greenery. Though it  was old, it looked charming. Mom told us this house belonged to Mr. and Mrs. Phùng-Xuân, parents of a former student of Mom's. They had kindly agreed to let us stay until we could find a place to settle down.

I looked at the house in awe. White lights gleamed through the door, illuminating a birdcage on the front porch. There was a faucet in the corner of the yard where someone was catching water to pour over the plants.

Clean water from the faucet was a luxury we could not afford during the eight years of living in dirt-floor huts, where we used oil lamps instead of electricity. I could not believe we were about to live in such a home, with bright electric lights and clean water from the tap whenever we wanted!

Mom knocked on a tall metal gate, and an older man opened it. He gave Mom a warm, welcoming smile and waved for us to all step in. The whole family came out to greet us.

They seemed very respectful to Mom and friendly to us. There were already nine people living in the house. I felt grateful for their generosity, as they were willing to take us in even though their home was already full.

The top floor of the house was a narrow hall with rows of beds. Two additional beds had been arranged for our family to use.

Sketch of the top floor of the house, from Mina's diary, 1982

During that period, we were required to have proof of permanent residency registration to remain in the city, which was impossible to apply for. Mom bribed the neighborhood guards, convincing them to let us stay temporarily. The next task was registering us at local schools, which Mom found even more difficult. Admission to these schools also demanded paperwork affirming our permanent residency.

Fortunately, another Mom's former student, Mr. Đỗ Duy Ngọc, a high school teacher in the city, came to our aid. Through additional bribes to local authorities, Mr. Ngọc brought us counterfeit documents that verified our legal residency. With his connections and more financial incentives, Mom successfully enrolled us in schools. As previously mentioned, as exceptional teachers, Mom and Dad earned their students' affection. Some students seemed to step in whenever we needed help, making things easier.

Homelessness

During our first few years living in Sài Gòn, we constantly moved from one place to another. There were too many of us for anyone to help for an extended period. Some of us were entering our teenage years, and dealing with teenagers is never easy.

We learned to keep our belongings small. We each had two bags that fit our clothes, books, and all other personal needs. It could be months, weeks, or even days when Mom told us to pack up to move. We quickly gathered our things and got ready to leave within hours. This happened so often that we stopped asking questions and let Mom take care of these matters. Somehow, through people she knew, Mom always found us a place to stay, even briefly.

Sketch of the corner of the older woman's place, from Mina's diary, 1983

On one occasion, Mom excitedly told us she found us an excellent place to stay. An older woman promised Mom we could rent the second floor of her house and took Mom's money. However, when six of us arrived, we found that the older woman had lied to us. She tried to rent out the room that some other tenants still occupied. As a result, we had to camp in the corner of the ground floor, sharing the room with the older woman. We spread a straw mat on the floor to sleep at night, and all our belongings were stuffed in bags piling around us.

The older woman was drunk most of the time, constantly yelling and shouting about things no one could understand. She also had a bird that squawked as loud as her. They screamed at each other nonstop all day long, and it felt as if we were living in a mental institution.

Seeing that the situation was miserable and stressful and that we could no longer stay at the place, Mom frantically biked around the city to find another home. For our lunch and dinner, Mom asked Aunt Dì Út to help  us while Mom searched for a place. Being used to challenging situations before, Dì Út got some firewood from the market, set up a cheap terracotta stove in the alley by the house, put a pot on top, and cooked us some rice soup or other simple dishes. She made things look so easy and always smiled at us, making us feel better despite our dreadful circumstances.

At the time, I was studying for my final ninth-grade exams and found it very hard to concentrate with all the drunk screaming and birds squawking all day. So, I would get up at 5 a.m. and walk to a friend's house to study with her. Being stressed, I often studied for the exam with tears streaming down, with my friend beside me awkwardly and quietly giving me a look of sympathy.

 My youngest sister, Mi-Nhon, always curled up on the mat and read her books during those days. That was her way of coping with stress and challenging times. My younger brother Lĩnh would play his guitar for hours, ignoring all the constant shouting from the drunk woman and the insane bird.

On the other hand, my youngest brother, Yên, would happily play with the street kids in the alleys after school. Many alleys in the city were usually filled with kids, mostly boys. They would noisily hang out, play games, fight, chase dogs and cats, kick cans like soccer balls, etc. Yên often did not come home for dinner, which worried Mom. My older sister Nu always biked around to look for him and brought him home.

Other times, Yên came home with bloody knees, a bruised face, black eyes, or a bumped head. His stories were always the same when asked: He fought against bullies to defend himself and his friends. He said he learned quick lessons about using his big head to bump into the opponent and fight them off like a bull, but he also knew when to run! Because of that, my brother earned his "street names" Bull Head and Big Head.

Another place we stayed was a tiny den of a house in the middle of an open market. From morning until evening, the market was bustling with people. Women sold baskets of fish flopping up and down, gasping for air. Men hung chunks of meat, bright red and still dripping blood, on metal hooks. Others spread newspapers on the ground and displayed fruits and vegetables to sell. There were carts with steaming pots of different kinds of dishes surrounded by people who squatted on the sidewalk, splurging their food. We usually could only watch these food carts from far away, secretly dreaming of tasting what smelled so good.

To get to our place, we would tiptoe on slabs of stone to avoid stepping on the muddy ground, soaked with dirty water and trash dumped onto the street by merchants.

Our den was tiny, enough to fit two twin-sized wooden counters that served as tables during the day and beds for six of us at night.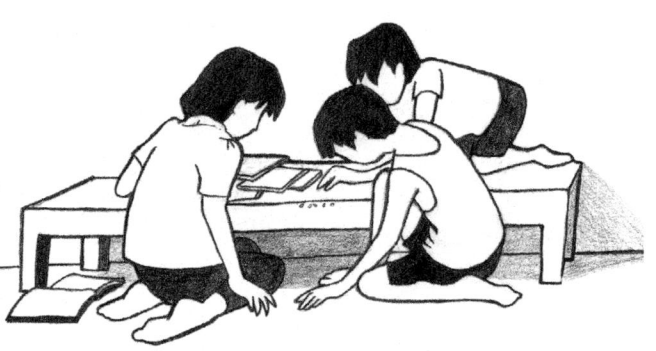
We usually sat on the floor to do homework at the counter, and when we rested our arms on the edge of the counter, we were bitten by tiny bedbugs that hid along the sides. Eventually, Mom bought some spray solution to treat the bugs. However, the spray was so strong that we gagged for days.

The worst part of that house was the washroom. I took turns with my sister Nu to hand-wash the family's laundry. Even during the day, it was dark in that room where the cockroaches always roamed freely. When doing laundry, I soaked all the clothes in buckets of soapy water for an hour or so. Then, after rubbing the clothes with a brush, I rinsed them with water and twisted them to squeeze all the excess water out before hanging them on the rooftop, where the owner of the house raised pigs to earn extra income. It usually took about a couple of hours or so to finish the laundry task. During that time, I always feared the cockroaches would get to me. I screamed and jumped when I felt something fly and brush against me. I was so happy when Mom told us to pack and move to the next place.

This time, we moved into a small garage that the owner turned into a room for rent. There were no cockroaches or bedbugs in this place. However, the septic-tank toilet we shared with the owner's family was constantly clogged. Moreover, the garage roof was constructed with metal sheets; therefore, our room sweltered like an oven during the day. Fortunately, shortly later, Mom ran into a friend and invited her to visit us. Seeing the bleak condition that we lived in, Mrs. Hoàng Hương Thuỷ felt terrible for our family. She had a house with two empty storage rooms in the back and offered to rent them to us.

Mrs. Thuỷ's place was a charming French-style house on a quiet, tree-lined street in an upscale neighborhood. Inside the tall fence that separated the house from a busy street nearby, fruit trees lined the spacious yard. The walkway was neatly covered with pebbles. Each of the two small brick rooms in the backyard could fit a queen-sized bed, perfect for the six of us to share. Mrs. Thuỷ had two daughters the same age as Nu and me, and we got along most of the time.

Every morning, I walked for thirty minutes to get to my high school, Lê Quý Đôn, where Nu also attended. Eventually, a kind friend in my class named Hồng Hà gave me a ride to school on the back of her bicycle. When Mom saved enough money to buy me a bike, Hồng Hà spent weeks teaching me how to ride it.

We lived there for about three years. By then, Nu and I had finished high school. We had made many good friends at that school who liked to visit us often. Understandably, the growth of the constant crowd and the happy young adults' noise became too much for Mrs. Thuỷ. Eventually, we were told to find another place to stay.

A Sweet Temporary Home

Sometimes, things came at the right time, as if God had planned them for us. Learning that our family was again searching for a place to stay, Hải, a close friend of my brother Lĩnh, told Lĩnh that his family had a small empty house for rent. The house was situated on the outskirts of the city, a bit farther from the center of Sài-Gòn yet still close enough for my younger siblings, Lĩnh, Yên, and Mi-Nhon, to bike to their schools.

When we packed our bags on top of our bicycles, we realized that after three years of staying put, we had accumulated more items than we had before. Luckily, our friends came to help, and after many bike trips under the boiling sun, we finally transported everything into our new home. For the first time in years, we now had a place we could call our own.

The little house sat at the end of a dirt road, shaded by thick tamarind trees that lined the whole neighborhood. We immediately fell in love with the peaceful area and our sweet new neighbors, mostly busy people from the working class who were probably as poor as we were.

We gazed at our new home. It was not much of a house; it was more like a brick shack with just two small rooms: a front room and a back room. The cement floor had cracks and holes. The tin roof flapped in the wind. The tropical  sun heated these tin roofs all year round and made the house swelter. And later when it rained, the roof would leak. We had to cover our mosquito net with plastic ponchos to stay dry at night. We placed pots and pans on the floor to catch the rainwater dripping through the roof.

The back of the shack stood on posts. It faced a blackish-looking pond that served as the community toilets and dumpster. During hot days, the smell from the pond was unbearable. In the rainy season, the water rises, bringing unpleasant things from the pond into our house.

Though we had tap water, there were often shortages, and the city would reduce the water supply to a minimum. We learned to keep the faucet open and let it drip into buckets through the night to have some water for the next day.

Despite the humble living conditions, we cherished our new home. This was the first time we had a place to ourselves. People could visit us anytime without bothering anyone else, and for the four years we lived there, we were happy. Our house was always crowded with visitors: aunts, uncles, cousins, and friends.

We had many friends, and Mom welcomed them all. I remember all the fun times we spent hanging out with them in that tiny shack. Though the smothering heat and constant attacks of mosquitoes were often unbearable, we still enjoyed our time together—playing games, singing songs, strumming on our guitars, and sharing stories. I remember lots of noise and mostly laughter. It was perfect!

When Aunt Huyền and her toddlers Bi and Ni stayed with us, we squeezed them in with no problems. "The more the merrier," Mom said.

My youngest sister, Mi-Nhon, found many friends in the neighborhood. After school, she curled up, read books, or played with the neighborhood children.

My younger brother Yên also built up his gang to have fun. Sometimes, he got in trouble with other kids, but thanks to God, he always came home in one piece! In the month leading up to Tết, the Vietnamese New Year, Yên decided to earn some money by crafting extra-large firecrackers, each one as wide as his arm. Our family had heard dreadful tales of individuals losing sight or even their lives from firecracker explosion accidents. He continued his "business" despite our efforts to dissuade him from creating such hazardous items. Miraculously, nothing unfortunate ever happened to Yên.

We had a very tight budget then. Our meals were simple and lean, and we often felt hungry. We constantly experienced migraines and stomachaches, likely due to chronic hunger. However, like most Vietnamese families, if someone visited us during our mealtime, we would bring out an extra bowl and a pair of chopsticks for our guests to join us. Of course, we would have to eat less, but we did not mind.

Nu made our clothes to save money, and she had a talent for this. As a teenager, I always felt self-conscious about my plain-looking garments. Nevertheless, Nu went to the market to find reasonably priced fabric. She skillfully helped me achieve a tidy and stylish appearance using an old-fashioned foot-operated sewing machine. Nobody could have guessed that we were experiencing financial difficulties. Additionally, many people assumed that, like other families anticipating reuniting with relatives overseas, we had substantial wealth!

Troublesome Paperwork

Our immigration paperwork took a long time. At the time, every legal authorization required some form of bribery. When the matter involved America, the amount of bribery needed was even more substantial, far beyond our financial means. Consequently, our file did not progress.

In America in 1985, Dad got a letter from the United Nations High Commissioner for Refugees (UNHCR). They informed him that his family in Vietnam was requested for an interview at their office in Sài-Gòn for American Visas. It seemed like the UNHCR also sent the same letter to the house we first stayed in when we moved to Sài-Gòn. Unfortunately, we might have already left the place, and the letter was never forwarded.

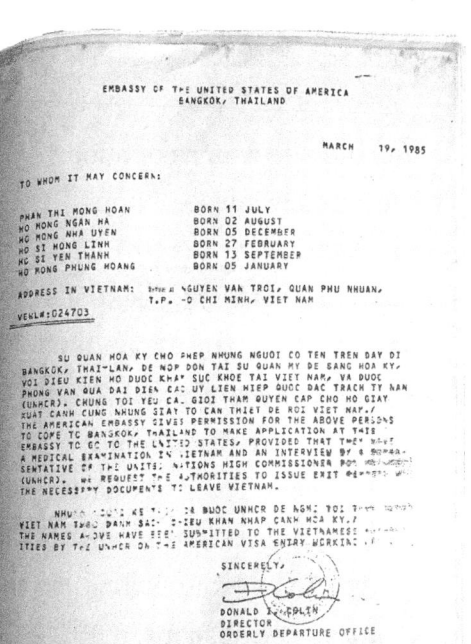

Maybe it got lost, or it could be that someone at the immigration office was waiting for us to show up and give them a large bribe.

We waited a long time to hear from the UNHCR. Months turned into years. It was frustrating and depressing. Nu and I finished high school but couldn't apply for college because of our uncertain status of "waiting to leave the country." It felt like we were stuck.

In late 1988, good fortune unexpectedly arrived. Mom ran into one of her former students, Mr. Nguyễn Chỉ, who resided in America but was visiting Vietnam for business. When Mom shared our years-long wait for a response from the UNHCR without any success, Mr. Chỉ kindly offered to help. He accompanied Mom to the UNHCR office in Sài-Gòn and urged them to locate our family's files. Mr. Chỉ's hefty bribes to the personnel and his American residency proved immensely helpful. When the search yielded no trace of our files, Mr. Chỉ spent significant money to initiate new files on our behalf.

After our file was re-opened, we felt a new surge of hope. While waiting for the UNHCR to contact us, we tried to make the most of our time by expanding our knowledge and skills. Even though we didn't have much money for food and clothes, somehow, amazingly, Mom still managed to pay for our English classes, music lessons, art, photography, and martial arts. Mom placed great value on art and education and wanted to prepare us for life in America, which we hoped would happen soon.

My First Solo Exhibition

Mom encouraged me to pursue my passion for art. After some searching, we were referred to take art classes with a well-known artist, Nguyễn Thị Tâm, who had a unique style of painting watercolors on silk. Her silk paintings were highly sought after by individuals preparing to emigrate abroad and wanted beautiful artworks from Vietnam to remind them of their homeland. I also received lessons in fundamental art theories from her late husband, the artist Nguyễn Long Sơn. I visited their small studio a few times a week, where I worked on drawing still life and painting on silk.

Mrs. Tâm's studio became my second home, where I could create art and meet many friends and talented artists. Creating art in this studio had a magical way of temporarily erasing all my troubles from my mind. Sometimes, we visited different cities to paint on location. I made lifelong friends with other classmates during this time, with whom I could reconnect and still keep in contact today, thanks to the social media and technologies of the 21st century.

Seeing that I made good progress in my art lessons, Mom allocated a modest budget and accompanied me on an extensive field trip in 1988. This journey allowed me to sketch and gather inspiration for my paintings. Mom brought me to Huế, her hometown, and Đà Nẵng, where I was born.

In Đà Nẵng, one of Mom's former students, Mr. Nguyễn Đình Xê, introduced us to the Hội-An's City Culture Manager, Mr. Hà Phước Mai. Mr. Mai and his wife, Hồng, warmly welcomed us into their home, treating us like their own family. During our visit to Hội An, we also met Mr. Võ Phùng, who worked with Mr. Mai. To ease the burden of our travel expenses, the two gentlemen arranged for us to stay at the city's guest house, a small room on the second floor of an antique wooden house on a quiet street in the ancient town.

Hội An was established in the fifteenth century as a significant trading port in Southeast Asia. Its weathered buildings reflected a beautiful blend of local and foreign influences from China, Japan, and Europe. Although it is now a bustling city crowded with tourists worldwide, it was quiet and deserted when I first arrived in 1988.

I instantly fell in love with the charming, narrow streets lined with uneven stones, surrounded by tiny houses with intricately tiled roofs covered in dark moss. Under the bright sun, I observed older women slowly walking down the streets, carrying heavy baskets of produce on their *gánh*—a bamboo pole slung over their shoulders with two baskets attached. With their delicate figures, these women demonstrated remarkable strength under their burdens.

Painting of Hội An by Mina Ferrante, 1989
Watercolor on silk

As night descended, the town seemed to fall asleep instantly. All the doors closed, and the streets became empty and quiet. Pale light peeked through the cracks of wooden windows, casting a gentle glow on the overgrown vines along the roads.

I spotted an older man pushing a cart, selling noodles in the quiet night. Occasionally, he tapped on a wooden pot, producing an echoing sound reverberating through the stillness. Steam rose from a hot pot at the center of his cart while the flickering light from the coal stove beneath revealed his tired, wrinkled face. Amidst the shadows of the ancient trees, the older man and the age-old street blended, creating a scene reminiscent of a silk painting, where the black ink had bled until everything appeared as a melancholic blur.

After leaving Hội An, we returned to Đà Nẵng. Mr. Nguyễn Đình Xê took us to visit the location where our house used to stand. Being there, where I was born and grew up, a rush of emotions flooded me. It had been thirteen years since we left this place, filled with unimaginable ups and downs for our family. Yet there I was, gazing at my birthplace, longing to relive its cherished memories again.

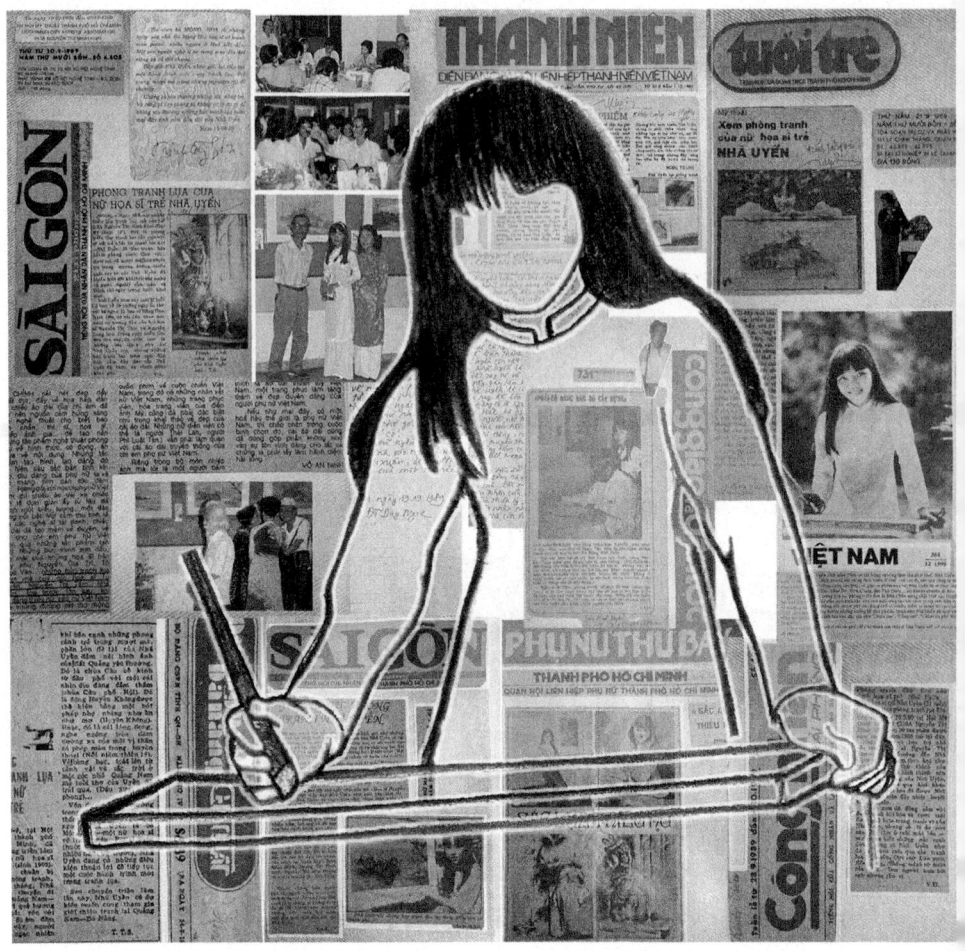

Inspired by the profound emotions gathered throughout my journey, I began working as soon as I returned to Sài Gòn. Over the next year, I completed 33 silk paintings. In August 1989, with the support of my mom, Mrs. Tâm, and friends in Sài Gòn—Mr. Nguyễn Thanh Bình, Mr. Bùi Nguyễn Trường Kiên, Mr. Vũ Duy Giang, and many others—I held my very first art solo exhibition at the city's Fine Art Association. The local newspaper recognized me as "Vietnam's youngest solo exhibition artist."

I was also honored that a family friend, Mr. Trịnh Công Sơn, a world-renowned Vietnamese songwriter, wrote an endorsement note for my exhibition brochure.

The Storm. by Mina Ferrante, 1989
Watercolor on silk

To express my gratitude to my hometown, I donated some proceeds to Quảng Nam City. The funds were utilized to aid the storm victims that damaged the area that year.

During the exhibition, I had the pleasure of meeting a remarkable business woman named Phấn. She was a successful entrepreneur and executive director at a prominent publisher in Vietnam. Alongside her publishing endeavors, she also invested in various businesses. Mrs. Phấn had a genuine passion for discovering young, aspiring artists and helping them on their path to success. She offered me a partnership

opportunity where I would create artwork on fabric to be sold to tourists at her stores. The customers then use the fabric to make traditional Vietnamese dresses called *áo dài*. The business thrived, allowing me to earn money and contribute to our household expenses.

The demand for painted silk fabric grew so high that I needed assistance from fellow artists. That was when I met Mr. Nguyễn Thanh Sơn, an incredibly talented artist. Like many people in

Vietnam then, Sơn faced challenges in finding work. Recognizing his talent and realizing I needed help, I approached Sơn and proposed a partnership. We rented out our next-door neighbor's front room and converted it into our studio. Then, we invited a few more artists to work with us.

These young artists, who joined after Sơn, were the people Mom and I met during my painting trip in Hoi An. They came to Sai Gon to make a living while applying to the city's Art University. When they visited us, Mom realized they were struggling financially. Hearing that the demand for the painted silk fabric was high, Mom suggested I offer them to work with me.

For several months, we created exquisite artwork on fabric that customers adored. Things were going very well; the customers kept us so busy we could barely keep up! The room we rented to work in was tiny. We worked on any surfaces we could find: table, bed, or floor. We worked hard all day and sometimes celebrated a good day with a drink in the evening at a little cafe down the street. Other times, Sơn and the boys picked up the guitar and sang their favorite songs. We were poor but high in spirit! The friendship I formed with Sơn and these young artists was something I cherished.

My brother Lĩnh still holds sweet memories of Sơn. Sơn occasionally invited him out for breakfast. Together, they would stroll up the dirt road to a small makeshift kitchen that a woman  set up every morning to sell a typical Vietnamese breakfast dish called *bánh cuốn*. They would squat on wooden stools and savor rolls of delicate, warm, steamed rice sheets served with lime and garlic fish sauce. On fortunate days, when Sơn had a bit of extra money from painting *áo dài*, he would treat himself and my brother to a few slices of *chả lụa*–a steamed pork cake–to embellish their meal. During that time, such a breakfast was a luxurious indulgence our family couldn't afford, making Lĩnh truly joyful whenever Sơn invited him to join.

During my solo art exhibition in August 1989, Mom ran into another former student, Mr. Huỳnh Bá Thành, who held a prominent position in Hồ Chí Minh City's police department. Seeing the difficult circumstances our family was living in deeply moved him. He reserved one of my silk paintings from the exhibition to show his support and asked Mom how else he could help. Mom mentioned that we were still waiting for our immigrant paperwork, which had been lost once, many years before. After Mr. Thành made several calls to ensure our case was handled correctly, we received a letter informing us that our visas had been granted. This allowed us to reunite with Dad in the U.S. Our family was soon called in for the American visa interview.

Six months later, our immigration papers were approved. I asked Sơn to take over the business and started preparing for our move to America. Sơn kept the shop running for a  few more years and eventually shut it down when the trend of painted *áo dài* faded. In time, Sơn made a name for himself in the art market, and now, more art collectors are looking to buy his paintings.

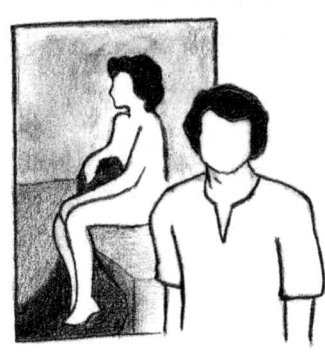 Some of the other young artists also are doing well. One of them, Bùi Tiến Tuấn, is now a high-profile artist in Vietnam, well known for his unique, stylized silk paintings. Đỗ Xuân Tịnh now teaches Art at Sài Gòn University and is financially stable in his career. Nguyễn Hữu Thấu, an artist in Hôi An, is happily relocated to Hungary with his family recently.

My achievements in Sài Gòn marked the first time I experienced personal success. I had built an image of myself as an individual, and it filled me with pride. Yet now, I had to leave it all behind because, after a decade of waiting, our family's long-held dream had finally come true.

We stood on the brink of a new chapter in life—a chapter that promised safety and opportunity, offering security after years of constant running and hiding. Despite the excitement, I couldn't help but feel anxious about the unknown as I hesitantly turned the page.

Chapter 11:
Together At Last

Making it in California

At the end of 1990, we flew from Vietnam to the United States. Dad thoroughly prepared for our arrival in San Jose, California, and rented a house that could accommodate all nine of us: Dad, Mom, six children, Uncle Huê, and his little puppy, Milky. The house had two bedrooms, two bathrooms, and a flat on the second floor. Though many were in the family, we made the most available space to ensure everyone's comfort.

In the backyard was a beautiful old maple tree as tall as our house. During the Fall, its leaves turned colors, creating a soft carpet of golden foliage. I could spend hours sitting on our sofa, gazing into the backyard, admiring the changing colors and weather. Finally, having our whole family under one roof brought me a sense of safety and happiness.

As soon as we arrived, Dad stressed the importance of education for our family, telling us it was the key to progress in America. Setting an example for us, at age 55, he was pursuing his Master's degree in Computer Science, taking one class at a time  each semester. He studied at night while working full-time as a computer engineer during the day. Thanks to his education and hardworking ethic, he survived many economic recessions in the Bay Area.

Dad encouraged my older sister, Nu, my brother, Lĩnh, and me to enroll in community colleges while Yên and Minhon started high school.

During those early days in America, we only spoke a little English. Out of all the hardships we had to encounter when moving to a new country, language was our biggest challenge. Thankfully, our oldest brother Tuyến had been in America with Dad since 1980 and thus could speak English fluently. He helped us throughout the process of getting settled in. He drove us to various places to complete the endless paperwork needed to establish our residency and register for schools. He also frequently ordered new food for us to try, and pizza became our favorite! I could never forget the first time I ate that warm, crunchy, savoring crust filled with hot, melting cheese!

After moving to the U.S. in 1980, Tuyến changed his name to Elwood to make it easier for others to pronounce and encouraged us to do the same. My sister Nu's official name, Ngân-Hà ("Milky Way"), symbolized the connection between our parents when they lived apart—Dad in Đà Nẵng, Mom in Huế. Though beautiful, it was hard for non-Vietnamese speakers, so she went with "Nu," from her nickname "Minu."

I was named Nhã-Uyển ("poetic garden") but now chose "Mina" as my official name, following her lead. My brother Hồng-Lĩnh, named after the mountain near Dad's hometown, became Frank. Another brother, Yên Thành, shortened his name to Yen. Our youngest sister, Phụng Hoàng ("Phoenix"), kept hers and now goes by Phoenix.

We lived in that cozy house for nearly a decade. While in school, we looked for part-time jobs to help with rent. Uncle Thuy kindly let Frank and Yen work with him on weekends in his growing gardening business.

Mai Liên—Elwood's then-girlfriend, now wife—helped Nu and me land jobs at Macy's. We thrived as diligent "runners," keeping the fitting rooms spotless and organized.

Art calls again

During this time, I tried to rekindle my passion for painting while waiting to start college. Reuniting with my family brought joy, but

starting over in a foreign land was tough. I deeply missed creating art—it felt like a part of me was missing.

Having just built up my reputation and business in Vietnam, leaving it all behind made the transition even harder. I missed both the income and the strong social network I had to abandon. That first year was rough—few friends, limited English, and no job.

Thankfully, our family, relatives, and friends offered invaluable support. Among them, Elwood's best friend, Phil, became a key supporter of my art. His encouragement motivated me to pursue an art career—he even drove me to art stores when I needed supplies. Phil also commissioned a set of hand-painted ties, and the earnings helped me stock up on materials.

Within a year, I created a collection of silk paintings and showcased them at the 1992 Tết Art Fair. Phil bought most of them for about $100 each, and those earnings were crucial in sustaining me until I got my first job at Macy's.

During the Tết Art Fair, a gentleman from the University of California, San Francisco (UCSF) stopped by my booth and was captivated by my silk paintings. Later, when UCSF's Health Department launched two health-promotion campaigns, he approached a San Jose ad firm with a special request: that I be commissioned to create the artwork for both projects over the next two years. One campaign promoted annual pap smears for early breast cancer detection, while the other encouraged smokers to quit.

Poster done for UCSF Health Department, 1992-1993

After I completed these projects, the advertising firm offered me a job as a graphic designer for their bi-monthly magazine, *Thị Trường Tự Do*. At the time, this publication

Drawing of a scene in AT&T's calling card advertising

was one of the most prominent Vietnamese magazines in the United States. Working at this advertising firm also led to an exciting opportunity—I landed a role in AT&T's television advertising for their calling cards. Incredibly, mobile phones were non-existent during that period, and people depended on phone cards for affordable long-distance calls from public booths or their homes. Witnessing the remarkable evolution of technology and its profound impact over time is truly astounding!

1994, I enrolled at the Academy of Art College (ACC) in San Francisco.

The Academy of Art College, Fine Art Building- oil painting by Mina Ho Ferrante 1994

During my third year at the ACC, I was chosen as one of 35 students recruited from 13 prestigious American, Canadian, and French art colleges to attend the Walt Disney Animation's Training Boot Camp.

Mina at the Disney Animation's Training Boot Camp in Montery, California- 1997

After completing the "Boot Camp," I was among the three students awarded a scholarship and a post-graduation opportunity to work for Disney Feature Animation Studios in 1998. During my five years at Walt Disney Animation, I worked as a layout artist, designing background sets for animated films such as Atlantis, Treasure Planet, Home on the Range, Tarzan 2, and Lilo and Stitch 2.

Sibling achievements

Elwood – When we reunited with my brother Elwood in America in 1990, he was nearly done with his computer engineering degree. Like many Vietnamese immigrants, he chose that field due to the high demand for tech jobs. But during his internship, he felt bored and unmotivated. Eventually, he quit and switched his major to advertising design at Academy of Art University in San Francisco, where he found real joy in creative work. Elwood's journey taught us to follow our passions when choosing a career. "When you're passionate about something, you'll excel at it," he said—and he proved it. He has previously worked for many companies such as GoPro, Intel and AMD. Today, he holds creative director position at a leading Silicon Valley tech company.

Elwood loves monster trucks and classic muscle cars and enjoys building them.

Beyond being smart and creative, Elwood has always been a caring brother, ready to help whenever we need him.

Nu – Taking Elwood's advice to heart, Nu decided to major in photography at AAC. During her final year at the art school, Nu  achieved first place in Mumm Cuvee's photography competition, earning her a one-year scholarship and a gallery show alongside some of the most renowned photographers. Following is a copy of Nu's award-winning photograph. It was a compilation of images created using early-day Photoshop techniques, then output

Nu's award-winning photograph in Mumm Cuvee's photography competition

onto film and contact-printed with an alternative photographic process, Palladium/Platinum printing, on Vietnamese organic silk.

In addition to her freelance photography work, Nu took computer graphics courses to enhance her skills as a freelance graphic designer. At AAC, She met Jack, a photography student who is now her husband.

After graduation, life took a new turn for Nu and Jack. They opened a neighborhood spot, Aunt Mary's Cafe, blending Southern American and Latin cuisines. The place quickly gained popularity in the East Bay

Illustration of Aunt Mary's Café by Song-An Zoe Stewart

and drew attention from top food magazines. It was even featured on the Food Network's TV show *Diners, Drive-Ins, and Dives* with Guy Fieri, cementing its status as a local favorite.

Since she was young, Nu has always cared for our family. Back in 1980, after Dad and Elwood escaped Vietnam, Mom frequently traveled to organize another boat trip to escape. Nu and the rest of us stayed on the farm with Uncle Hiệp. Like a

young mother, Nu managed the small fund Mom left for groceries, instructed us to gather roots and vegetables from our farm when the money ran low to prevent starvation, and tended to my brother Yên when he fell ill, which happened quite often.

Fast forward to 2017, after Mom had a heart attack and developed dementia, Nu would drive from Oakland weekly to help Dad take care of Mom. She made appointments, spoke with doctors and nurses, and handled endless paperwork from hospitals and insurance companies.

Mom passed away in 2020, leaving Dad behind. He's now nearly 90, fragile, mostly in bed, and living with advanced diabetes that has taken a toll on his health. Despite a demanding schedule—going back to school to major in ceramics—Nu constantly commutes between her home and Dad's to make sure his health is closely monitored. She watches over him like a hawk, feeding him and administering his medications with the skill of a nurse.

Even while caring for Dad, Nu stays closely connected with her siblings, checking in to make sure everyone is doing well and stepping in to help whenever needed. In our family, we affectionately call her "the Sword of Justice" for her straightforward, disciplined nature. But we all know that beneath that strong exterior is a soft, caring, and deeply loving heart.

Frank – My younger brother, Frank, pursued architecture at Cal Polytechnic State University in San Luis Obispo, California. After completing his studies, Frank opted to work as a freelance architect and consistently has a steady stream of projects. His clients adore his designs for their exquisite homes.

Not only is Frank talented in his field, but he also possesses excellent business acumen. He acquires dilapidated properties, renovates them, and sells them for a profit.

Frank is a diligent individual. He devotes time to constructing his own home when he's not working for clients or playing soccer with his friends on weekends. Over five years, he gradually transformed his modest house into an extraordinary architectural marvel. The home exudes a perfect balance of positive energy and serenity, creating a welcoming atmosphere as soon as one steps inside.

Frank's family, oil – by Mina Ho Ferrante, 2020

In our family, we playfully call Frank the "family bank." Since he was little, Frank has been excellent at saving money, no matter how little he has. At the same time, he doesn't hesitate to lend money to his siblings whenever anyone needs it, even when he's unsure if he can get any of his money back!

Yen – After graduating high school in 1993, my younger brother Yen joined the U.S. Army Reserve, specializing in combat medicine. Yen completed six months of training in Texas and continued to serve in the Army Reserve for six years, attending training sessions at the Oakland Army base in California once a month on weekends. During this time, Yen also took construction classes at community colleges.

Oil portrait of Yen, oil- by Mina Ho Ferrante, 1995

After leaving the Army Reserve, he started working as a carpenter. His team constructed frames for significant public projects, including major highways, sports stadiums, etc. Some notable projects include the underground sewer system for the Chase Arena, where the Golden State Warriors play, the stormwater pump station for Stanford University's football stadium, the Richmond Bay Area Rapid Transit station, and numerous maintenance holes in the Bay Area.

Eventually, Yen bought a property and skillfully built his dream home, which is spacious enough to accommodate his family of six and our parents comfortably. Currently, Yen works as a Combination Building Inspector for the city of San Jose's Public Work Department.

Yen's family, oil by Mina Ho Ferrante, 2019

On weekends, he, his wife Nam-Trân, and their four children actively participate in the Eucharistic Youth Movement. Yên and Nam Trân help teach Catholic doctrine and the Bible, creating enjoyable activities to make learning appealing to kids and assisting parents in building up their children's faith lives.

Yen says he was wild and reckless as a child but always felt our family's unconditional love, which acted as an anchor and guided him toward becoming a kind and caring person. This is why he is now passionate about helping young children, especially those who may be lost or troubled and need love and guidance, stay on the right path.

Phoenix – In 1994, my youngest sister, Phoenix, graduated from high school. She then pursued studies in International Business and later achieved two Masters degrees, one in Educational Leadership and Management and the other in Career Development Counseling. Initially, she worked as a career counselor at RMIT University in Vietnam, a branch of the Australian research university, Royal Melbourne Institute of Technology (RMIT). However, she eventually co-founded Sông An (Peaceful River) Career Development Social Enterprise, a leading organization in Vietnam specializing in career development education and guidance.

Phoenix is a bright and well-educated person, but what sets her apart is her caring and loving nature. She is passionate about helping and educating others, which shines through in everything she does. She is highly dedicated to her work in Vietnam and has become a trusted mentor to many young people. By shaping their careers, she makes a positive impact on their lives.

Phoenix is a career educator and counselor. Her main goal is to help workers find satisfaction at work and be ready to develop in the global market. Sông An Career Development Social Enterprise's vision is to empower learners and workers to self-guide their career development journey and find fulfillment and success.

Mom and Dad

In 1990, after Mom brought five of us to Dad in America, she jokingly said she had fulfilled her duties and could now focus on her dreams. Dad had promised to buy her a piano upon her arrival, and he kept his word. Mom started

playing the piano again, writing, and eventually self-publishing a few books. She also attended West Valley College with her children and earned her Associate degree in art. Even after graduating, she continued taking art classes  like painting, sculpture, and pottery, creating beautiful artwork.

Mom actively participated in Vietnamese organizations' events, auctioning her artwork and selling her books to support charity foundations, such as the one aiding an orphanage and a charity clinic in Nguyệt Biều Huế. These foundations were managed by nuns who were Mom's friends.

When she wasn't writing or sculpting, Mom spent time with her grandchildren and visited friends. She was witty, funny, and had a straightforward way of speaking. Everyone loved

her, including her family, friends, and students from over fifty years ago.

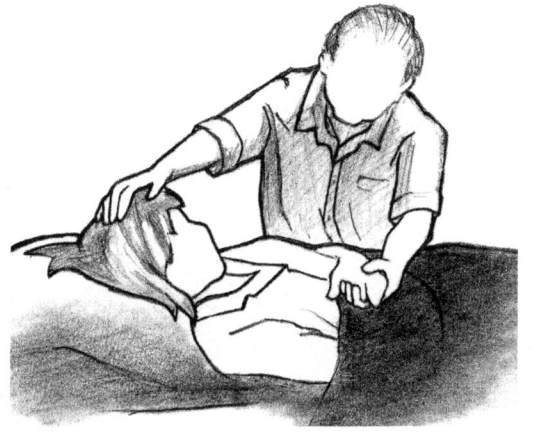

In September 2017, Mom suffered a major stroke and underwent open-heart surgery. Dad stayed by her side, comforting her during her unconscious days, gently stroking her hair, and whispering to her stories from the past and present.

Though she survived, dementia gradually affected her, removing her ability to move and talk. For three years, Dad lovingly cared for her, attending to all her needs, such as feeding, cleaning, and changing her diapers.

Mom passed away on August 18, 2020. I miss Mom every day, and I pray to her in challenging times. I still feel her strong presence, bringing me comfort and strength. Her memory lives on and remains an important part of my life.

Portrait of Mom, watercolor by Mina Ho Ferrante, 2020

As for Dad, in the late 1990s, after each of his children graduated college and pursued their dreams, Dad remained devotedly working as a computer engineer in San Jose; his companies recognized his intelligence and hard work.

Thanks to his hardworking ethic, Dad could always secure a job at a good company despite the widespread downsizing of multiple companies. Before his retirement in the early 2000s, he worked for Carco Inc., which made Flight Motion Simulators (FMS). Its clients included Lockheed Martin, aircraft companies, and the U.S. military. While working for Carco, Dad was occasionally sent to South Korea and Taiwan to set up the FMS for the clients there.

Portrait of Dad, watercolor by Mina Ho Ferrante, 2020

On the weekends, Dad actively participated in different organizations, volunteering to raise funds to help people in the Vietnamese community and church.

Dad was devastated after Mom was gone. For months, every corner of the house and everything he did would remind him of her, and he would break down in tears. He often flips through our family albums to look at Mom's pictures, and whenever

he talks about her, his eyes glitter with love and tenderness.

Dad lives in an add-on unit that Yen built for him, connected to his house. Every day, Yen's young children come by to give him hugs. Lately, Dad has been bedridden most of the time. But before that, he used to do light gardening as a form of exercise, and he loved watching the children play in the backyard—it always brought him joy.

On the walls of his living room, Dad fills them up with Mom's pictures and the paintings she created while she was alive. One could see that the story of Mom's life surrounds Dad.

Only about a year ago, when Dad could still walk well, he and Nu often visited the cemetery where Mom was laid to rest, just a few blocks from his home. Dad would light a few incense sticks for Mom, then quietly sit by her grave.

I once accompanied Dad to the cemetery a little before sunset, and we sat silently next to Mom's gravestone for a while. He seemed lost in his own world. Then, Dad softly uttered some  words, and I wasn't sure if they were meant for me, himself, or Mom: "I wonder how it will be when we get to the other side of this world."

Caught off guard, I had no consolation to offer him. We continued to sit until the golden light at the horizon turned to soft lavender. Eventually, I followed Dad as he slowly walked home, his frail figure blending into the grayish twilight.

These days, we treasure our time with Dad. Since Mom's passing—and even before his health began to decline—Dad has gradually withdrawn from community activities and feels somewhat detached from the lively  social life he once had. Still, his friends and former students reach out through phone calls, emails, and the occasional visit.

Despite a difficult past, Dad remains kind, honorable, and deeply spiritual. He continues to love and give selflessly every day. Throughout his hardworking life—and even now in his modest retirement—he's generously supported others, often sending money each month to those in need, especially young people pursuing their dreams through education.

While witnessing the physical toll on my parent is heart-wrenching, it brings solace knowing that Dad is embraced by comfort and affection in his later years. After a life scarred by immense hardships, he has finally found peace, allowing his children to reciprocate the care he so selflessly gave.

Dad is our guide, idol, and hero to us, his children. He is the inspiration behind this book—a rose that thrives in a harsh environment and continues to give to life every day it blooms. Thanks to Dad, we hope to learn from him and become roses from the crimson rocks ourselves.

Epilogue

Our big family gathering in Tet 2024

This chapter is written for family members to catch up on recent updates about one another. Other readers may find it too detailed and might choose to skip it.

The family thrives

For decades, I reveled in the strong bonds of our intergenerational family. Most of us lived in nearby cities, leading to frequent family gatherings filled with many uncles, aunts, and countless cousins, to the point where names were challenging to keep track of.

Summers were marked by camping trips that often included friends, in-laws, dates, and extended family. My parents actively participated in these events, watching over the younger generation while we, their adult children, managed other tasks. It was a time of comfort and support, and I never imagined these joyous gatherings would someday cease.

Over the years, we've experienced many losses. My mother, along with several aunts and uncles, has passed away. Many of my cousins have moved to Texas due to California's rising cost of living. My father, now almost 90 and managing high blood pressure and diabetes, has slowed down significantly. His days mostly consist of sleeping, eating, watching a bit of news on his computer, and then heading back to bed.

My brother Yen and his wife, Tran, built an adjoining living space for Dad so he could stay close, and Yen's young children often keep him company. Nu constantly watches over Dad, while my other brother Frank's wife, An, prepares weekly batches of easily reheated meals for him. To monitor his well-being, we installed a kitchen camera, and he carries a device that alerts us if his blood sugar levels fluctuate, allowing us to check in on him.

Although I moved to Southern California after my marriage in 2000, I try to fly back and visit Dad every few months. This living arrangement has prevented Dad from succumbing to the isolation many elderly Americans face.

Dad's life in America

Dad and his brother, Uncle Thuy, have lived near each other in San Jose, California, since they fled the harsh Vietnamese regime in 1980. While Dad pursued his education, Uncle Thuy and Aunt Lệ built a gardening and landscaping business.

As soon as their finances allowed, Uncle Thuy and Dad extended their support to their siblings and relatives in Vietnam, providing financial aid and emotional solace. They also actively engaged in their churches and other community groups in San Jose. Together with their brothers and sisters, they work to heal wounds of the past. The pain of losing their parents in such a tragic and unjust way will always be there; however, with love between the siblings, they can help each other move on and pave for a more tranquil life.

In 2000, Mom and Dad returned to Vietnam to attend Phoenix's wedding in Sài Gòn. During their visit, they explored various cities. This was Dad's first and only return to Vietnam since his departure in 1980.

The most poignant moment of their trip was the reunion with Dad's long-separated siblings in Nghệ-An, whom he had bid farewell to more than half a century ago. Emotions—both sadness and joy—filled the air as the brothers and sisters embraced again. They shared the stories and relived the pain of their past, yet, in each other's company, they found solace and dried each other's tears.

Since Dad left in 1958, his siblings eagerly awaited seeing him again. They spoke of Dad with deep love and admiration. He had been the family's beacon of hope, a source of strength and inspiration in adversity. They longed for the day Dad would return, proudly restoring the family's honor and status.

Dad united with his siblings in Nghệ An in 2000

Setting examples through the generations

In their prime, Dad and Mom were active volunteers in various Vietnamese community associations in San Jose. After Mom's passing, Dad, now frail, withdrew from community activities, feeling somewhat isolated from his former social circle. However, his friends and former students still maintain contact through phone calls and emails. While witnessing my parent's physical decline is saddening, it's comforting to know that Dad is spending his twilight years in comfort and care. After a life marked by extreme hardships, he can finally rest and allow his children to care for him.

What brings Dad the most happiness is his ability to continue supporting his family, relatives, and society. He has been carefully managed a modest income from monthly social security checks. He contributes to his household expenses, gives monetary gifts to his grandchildren on special occasions, and sets aside funds to support struggling relatives in Vietnam, helping them complete their education and secure employment. Dad also regularly contributes to charitable organizations and foundations that aid the less fortunate or provide disaster relief.

While caring for Dad, my siblings, cousins, and I also try our best to reach out to our other elderly relatives. Our frail Uncle Huệ in San Jose receives occasional visits and lunch outings to alleviate his growing loneliness, as he drives less to see his friends and relatives. During holiday gatherings, we invite aunts, uncles, and cousins, maintaining the bonds of our extended family. These moments warm our hearts.

Additionally, we occasionally provide financial assistance to our elderly relatives in Vietnam, especially during times of illness when medical bills weigh heavily on them. Thanks to the cultural tradition that younger generations must care for their elders, these relatives may not be isolated living in their multi-generational households, but financial support remains critical.

Most of us are now in our 50s; my siblings and I understand the aging process and the circle of life better. We cherish the emotional support of our intergenerational family and strive to instill these values in our children. The future remains uncertain, and whether the younger generation will care for us as we care for our elders is still being determined. Nevertheless, we can only hope that our actions serve as an example, teaching our children to do the right thing by actually doing it. The following are some updates about my family and relatives, with some illustrations done by the younger artists in our clan.

DAD'S FAMILY

O Hồ Thị Thiệu

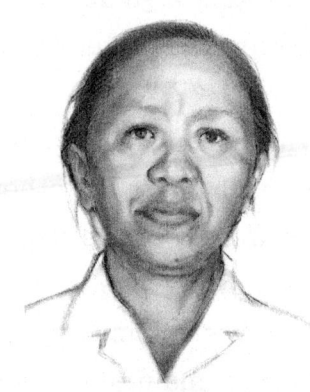

O Thiệu, Dad's oldest sister, passed away in 2016, leaving behind her four children —Thái Duy Thức, Thái Duy Thắng, Thái Thị Trâm, and Thái Thị Liên—along with four sons and daughters-in-law, many grandchildren, and great-grandchildren. My cousin Trâm's daughter, Lê Thanh Hà, lives in San Jose. She is a registered nurse and was crucial in caring for Mom during her final years. As Mom was bedridden and needed constant medical attention, Hà regularly checked in on Mom, coordinated her care, provided us with medical advice, and offered emotional support during this difficult time. Our family truly appreciated her dedication and kindness.

O Hồ Thị Tiệu

O Tiệu, Dad's older sister, is now 93 years old and lives in Nghệ-An. She has five daughters—Hoàng Thị Tâm, Hoàng Thị Minh, Hoàng Thị Bình, Hoàng Thị Phương, and Hoàng thị Liên—and many grandchildren and great-grandchildren.

O Hồ Thị Tạo

O Tạo, Dad's older sister, passed away in 1980. She was survived by six children and many grandchildren and great-grandchildren. Her children are: Đào Thị Lương, Đào Thị Hoa, Đào Văn Khôi, Đào Thị Thuận, Đào Thị Hiền, and Đào Văn Đồng.

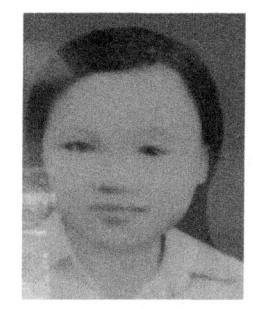

O Hồ Thị Mỹ

O Mỹ is Dad's younger sister. She lives in Đà Nẵng, Vietnam. She has four children—Trần Thị Dung, Trần Thị Hà, Trần Ngọc Liên and Trần Ngọc Hoàng— many grand children and great-grandchildren.

Uncle Hồ Sĩ Thuy

Uncle Thuy was Dad's younger brother. After 1975, he left Nghệ An and settled in Rạch Giá, near Dad. When their plan to escape Vietnam together fell through and Dad had already left, Uncle Thuy came up with his own solution and managed to cross the ocean to Thailand, as recounted in Chapter 8.

In the United States, Uncle Thuy settled in San Jose with Dad. They maintained a strong bond. Uncle Thuy and Aunt Lệ eventually established a landscaping and gardening business. They worked tirelessly day and night, raising their six children, all of whom have become successful adults with good jobs; some have beautiful families.

In his 60s, freed from financial concerns, Uncle Thuỵ returned to school, enrolling in English courses to document his memories of life in Vietnam. He also continued to work part-time to stave off boredom.

In July 2019, while trimming a tree for a client, Uncle Thuỵ fell from a ladder. He later passed away in the hospital without the chance to say goodbye to his loved ones. His adult children remain close and lovingly care for their mother. Uncle Thuỵ and Aunt Lệ have six children—Cindy, Mary, Mai-Anh, Terri, Paul, and Elizabeth—and many grandchildren.

His wife, Aunt Lệ, continues to manage the gardening company. On weekends, she spends time with her grandchildren. Aunt Lệ is known for her generosity towards her relatives, regularly sending money to support those in need in Vietnam.

O Hồ Thị Mìều

O Mìều is Dad's youngest sister. She lives in Nghệ-An. Her husband passed away in 2020. She has six children—Nguyễn thị Yến, Nguyễn Văn Cảnh, Nguyễn thị Cẩm, Nguyễn Xuân Cương, Nguyễn thị Phương, and Nguyễn thị Tuệ—and many grandchildren and great-grandchildren. At present, Cảnh, Cương, and Tuệ live in America.

Uncle Hồ Sĩ Lĩnh

Uncle Lĩnh is Dad's youngest brother. He lives in NghệAn with his wife, Nguyễn thị Khương. They have seven children—Hồ thị Thanh, Hồ thị Nhàn, Hồ Sĩ Quý, Hồ thị Thảo, Hồ Sĩ Thoả, Hồ thị Thuần, and Hồ Hoàng Nhuy—and many grandchildren.

In 2010, Dad sponsored Nhuy to immigrate to America, with the accompaniment of Uncle Lĩnh and Aunt Khương. After briefly living in the U.S., Uncle Lĩnh and Aunt Khương found that they did not fit in with the lifestyle in America. They missed the way of living they had been accustomed to, and they missed the extensive support system of family, relatives, and friends from the close-knit community they left in Vietnam. Most of all, they felt the responsibility of regularly tending to the ancestors' altar back home. They also missed the open countryside air where they had resided before coming to America. Therefore, Uncle Lĩnh and Aunt Khương only stayed in America for a few years and decided to return to their hometown of Nghệ-An. Nhuy and their other adult children reside in different countries, including America, England, Austria, and Germany.

Currently, Quý resides in Germany, Thoả is in England, Thuần is in Austria, and Nhuy lives in America.

The family of Grandfather's second wife

My cousin, Mr. Thái Duy Thức, the oldest son of Dad's oldest sister, O Hồ Thị Thiệu, provided me with this additional information as follows.

Grandfather's family was the wealthiest in the region, yet for the first nine years of their marriage, Grandmother only gave birth to three daughters. In those days, under the strict customs of feudalism, a man needed a son to carry on the family name. Because of this, Grandfather married a second wife, hoping for a male heir.

Cousin Thái Duy Thức in Hanoi

The second wife was Bà Võ Thị Phượng. She had three children with Grandfather: Hồ Thị Loan, a daughter who was older than Dad; Hồ Sĩ Mại, a son younger than Dad; and Hồ Sĩ Mao, a son younger than Uncle Thuy. Loan, Mại, and Mao have all passed away. Inevitably, when there were two wives in a family, conflicts arose. It worsened as both women, competing for the title of "lady of the house," raced to bear a son before the other. Then, when Grandma gave birth to Dad before Bà Phượng gave birth to Uncle Mại, Grandma secured her title and position in the household.

It wasn't until the past few years, when the children of the second wife had passed away, that the grandchildren and great-grandchildren of both women began to connect more peacefully.

I found Mr. Thức's information essential and valuable. It helps younger generations understand the context of a period when feudalism transitioned to communism and how Grandpa's family, one of the wealthiest farming families in the region, got caught in the storm. Therefore, despite some sad memories that no one wants to remember, Dad and Mr. Thức advised me to include these stories in this book as part of our family record.

MOM'S FAMILY

Uncle Hiệp

Uncle Hiệp passed away in 1985 at age 48, leaving behind his wife, Trần Thị Hoa, daughters Hoài Hương and Hoài Phương, and sons Dân Việt, Dân Nam, and Quốc Cường. He was also survived by children-in-law and nine grandchildren. Most of them reside in Texas and lead financially comfortable and good lives.

Aunt Mộng Hoà

Aunt Hoà passed away in 2023. She left behind five children: Trương Minh Mộng-Tuyền, Trương Minh Anh-Tuấn, Trương Minh Cát-Tín, Trương Minh Hiếu-Toàn, Trương Minh Nhật-Tân, Trương Minh Nhất-Tiến, and Trương Minh Nhã Tiên, as well as seven daughters- and sons-in-law, 18 grandchildren, and two great-grandchildren.

Cousin Mộng Tuyền's family

Mộng Tuyền, the oldest child of Aunt Mộng Hoà, wrote the following passages: "I earned the nickname "Calamity" when I was young, likely because of my stubborn and challenging nature. Ironically, I've spent 16 years as a preschool teacher, where staying sweet and patient with young children is essential. I have three adult children—two daughters and a son, all leading independent lives. My son has a family with two children, a boy and a girl. While my family resides in Vietnam, my siblings live in the U.S.

Although I've never had a leisurely day, I genuinely appreciate what I have. I recognize that, compared to many people around me, I am in a much better situation. Since my mother passed away, I feel like I've lost a significant part of my life. I miss her daily, especially when dusting her picture on the family altar. I still hear her talking to me, gentle laughter, and comforting conversations. I pray to her for protection over my family.

Reflecting on my journey, I see that there have been good and bad days. However, I'm grateful to God for always being with me and for the people who have stood by me through thick and thin."

Cousin Cát-Tín family
Cát-Tín is Aunt Mộng Hoà's third child. Uyên Võ, Cát-Tín's wife, wrote this passage: "I'm Uyên Võ, the fourth daughter-in-law of Má Mộng-Hoà. Since I was young, I've had a deep passion for cooking and love crafting delicious dishes for others to enjoy. I work at a hot pot restaurant—a job I truly enjoy. My husband is Tín Trương, with whom I've spent a lifetime arguing about all kinds of things. Still, I hold him close in my heart as a genuinely good man, and I take pride in his talent for remodeling homes and workspaces.

Illustration by Anh Trương (aka Mia), 12 years old.
Anh Trương is Cát-Tín's daughter.

We have three children. Our eldest, Nghi Trương, is 18. She's hardworking, supporting herself while chasing her dream of becoming a nurse. Her sweet, friendly nature makes her well-loved. Our second daughter, Anh Trương, is 12. Though she can be blunt, she has a compassionate heart. She dreams of becoming an interior designer, using her art to enhance living spaces. The youngest, our son Khoa Trương, is eight. He's full of love and care, always asking how we're doing.

Our future happiness centers around our children. We often whisper to them, "Always be a good person before becoming a talented one."

Cousin Hiếu-Toàn's family

Hiếu-Toàn is the fourth child of Aunt Mộng Hoà. An Truong, aka Xoay, the oldest child of Hiếu-Toàn, wrote this passage: "Our family of four consists of my dad, Toàn (or Andrew), my mom, Phượng (she goes by Kathy for business), my 17-year-old brother, Trung (a.k.a. Sam to family or those close to him), and me, An (nicknamed Xoay in my family).

Illustration by An Trương

My dad works at Western Digital and has always been passionate about athletics. He recently added swimming to his morning routine, which he is proud of. My mom finds joy in tending to her garden, constantly expanding her collection of flower pots, watching dramas, and reaching out to friends and relatives when she's not working hard. Sam is a League of Legends connoisseur (currently Diamond 4) and is also a dedicated gym and fitness enthusiast. He is ambitious and aspires to one day provide for those in need.

I'm a psychology sophomore at Ohlone College who aims to transfer to UC San Diego to pursue a bachelor's degree in cognitive science! I relish spending time with my family, friends, and dog, Ramen (whom I should've included in our family roster), going to the gym, and working on personal growth. I hope to do at least three pull-ups by reading this in a published book."

Cousin Nhất-Tiến's family

Nhất-Tiến is the sixth child of Aunt Mộng Hoà. In 2024, Tiến and his family moved from California to Texas. The eldest child, Minh (as known as Chích-Bông), wrote this following passage: "June 1st, 2023 was the day our family arrived in Katy, Texas. The new adjustment was a big change, spending more fun and valuable time together. This family puts on new challenges for a better life in Texas. The household consists of five people and one silly dog. Alex, the second born, is always looking forward to learning new things. Jesse, who is the youngest child, is considered to be very helpful amoungst the family. Minh, the first born, is heading into her teenage years and works to do academically well in school. This lovely family lives among the lines of "Life is beautiful, enjoy every moment alongside other living beings. Chích Bông, 10/28/2023"

And here is what Alex wrote: "Family! Hello! I'm Alex and I'm the 2nd child in my family, And my life is really fun 'cause me and my family got to go to Missouri, Florda, and Mexico, And a fact is that me and my family love ead and another. Sincerely, Alex"

Illustrations by Chích Bông (Minh) and Alex

Cousin Nhã-Tiên's family

Nhã-Tiên, the youngest child of Aunt Mộng Hoà, wrote this passage: "We've lived in the U.S. for 11 years, three years in California and eight years in Texas. We cherish every moment in our lives, both the happy and the sad. With three sons, we've given them Vietnamese names, ensuring they always remember their roots. We operate a small store that sells clearance items to local customers and provides services to the Vietnamese community. Our eldest child is in 8th grade and dreams of attending Texas A&M University. Our second child is in 1st grade, and the youngest is studying in Kindergarten in Katy City, Texas. We are proud of our hard work and the independence it affords us. Our goal is to earn enough money while also having more time for our family.

Our ultimate dream is to explore all 50 states together and travel to various countries worldwide. We want to experience the world's vastness and appreciate the beauty Mother Nature has bestowed upon humanity."

Illustration by 5 years old Đan Nguyễn, Nhã-Tiên's son.

by Đan Nguyễn (5 years old)

Aunt Hằng

Aunt Hằng's husband, Nguyễn Hữu Thu, passed away in 1991, and Aunt Hằng passed away in 2023, leaving behind her four children—Hoàng-Vũ, Tri-Túc, Hoàng-Nhân, and Tri-Tâm —along with many grandchildren. Túc, Nhân, and Tâm's families reside in Vietnam, while Vũ's family lives in Texas.

Tri-Túc, the older daughter of Aunt Mộng Hằng, wrote this passage: "Maria Mộng Hoa, a talented female artist from Huế, was my grandmother. Just hearing her name fills me with pride! Although I didn't have the chance to live near her for long, her image always remains vivid whenever I think of her. She was a beautiful, gentle, and gracious woman. People often say, "Like mother, like daughter," but in my case, being the granddaughter of her sixth daughter (Mộng Hằng), I didn't inherit her beauty or personality traits, but that's all right. No matter what, I proudly bear the title of the granddaughter of a gifted artist. Maria Mộng Hoa was a woman of artistic brilliance and integrity, and I always take pride in sharing her story with others!"

Uncle Huệ

Uncle Huệ now lives in San Jose, California, with his sweet puppy dog, Mít, and two birds he adores. He finds peace in living in a small house with a tiny backyard, flourished with fragrant blooms. On the weekends, he enjoys going to flea markets or garage sales to buy little antique knick-knacks that he gives to his nieces and nephews when they visit him. Once in a while, he calls and visits Dad, and they talk about the old days. He's always been such a sweet man.

Aunt Mộng-Hài

Following Grandma's passing in 1986, Aunt Hài had two children. Unfortunately, Aunt Hài experienced a stroke and passed away in 2016. She is survived by her son, Phan Phước Vĩnh Hiền, her daughter, Công Huyền Tôn Nữ Thanh Hải (Lisa), and three grandchildren – Jolie, Josiah, and John. Hiền resides in California, while Hải's family lives in Texas. Both have stable jobs and lead comfortable lives.

Aunt Mộng-Huyền

Aunt Mộng-Huyền currently resides in Texas with her puppy Cali. Sadly, her late husband, Trần Thanh-Bình, passed away in November 2023. Aunt Mộng-Huyền has two children: Nguyễn Phan Thiên-Ân, a nuclear engineer, and Nguyễn Phan Mộng Quỳnh-Uyển, a pediatrician. She also has a granddaughter named Elsie Âu Cơ Smith and a grandson named Wren An Nguyễn.

Cousin Thiên-Ân

Thiên-An, the oldest child of Aunt Mộng Huyền, wrote this passage: "Thiên-An and Thảo-Uyên live in San Jose with their two cats, Boba and Miutea, and a dog, Helen. Uyên recently graduated and is pursuing a career in digital media. Thiên-An likes to garden and grill. We love to spend our weekends cooking great meals or exploring local

Illustration by Châu Thảo-Uyên, (aka Thi Chau), Thiên-An's wife

cafes and restaurants." 2023, Thiên-An and Thảo-Uyên welcomed their newborn son, Wren An Nguyễn.

Cousin Quỳnh-Uyển (aka Ni, or Quynh)
Quỳnh-Uyển, the youngest child of Aunt Mộng Huyền, wrote this passage: Ni (Quynh) and her husband, Josh, live in Alameda, California. Ni is a pediatrician, and Josh is a pharmacist. They have a daughter named Elsie and two dogs, Lucy and Ethel. They all enjoy traveling, food, and hiking.

Illustration by Aunt Huyền

Uncle Bê-Em

Uncle Bê-Em resides in Rạch-Giá, Vietnam, with his wife, Kim-Oanh. They are parents to two children, Phạm Duy-Anh and Phạm Thiên-An, and proud grandparents to two grandchildren, Thiên-Anh and Hải-Đăng. His son Duy-Anh is also an amazing graphic artist. What's even more exciting is that Uncle Bê-Em is one of the illustrators in this book!

Uncle Út Hậu

Uncle Út Hậu lived in Phú Quốc, Kiên Giang, with his wife Mỹ-Lệ. Uncle Hậu peacefully passed away in May 2024 and was survived by his loving wife, two daughters, and three granddaughters.

Aunt Mộng-Hoài

Aunt Hoài, also known as Dì Út, resides in San Jose with her two sons, Phùng Đăng-Khoa and Phùng Hoài-Nam. Her dedication lies in maintaining a healthy and physically fit lifestyle, embracing balanced meals and daily yoga practice.

MINA'S FAMILY

Mina

I married Joseph Ferrante, a podiatrist, in 2000. Although I enjoyed my work at Walt Disney Animation Studio, I chose to step back and prioritize being a full-time mother to my three young children, Micangelo (Mic), Angelina, and Joseph-Paul (JP).

When the children were young and attending elementary school, I volunteered to be near them at their school. A few hours of helping teachers with tasks like making copies or decorating classrooms eventually became full-time involvement. I actively participated in PTA meetings and fundraising events, taught photography and art classes, initiated an art club where approximately 500 children took turns creating art during lunchtime, and spearheaded the creation of a mural that allowed all the students in the school to participate in painting and sign their names at the end.

As my youngest son moved on to middle school, I also began rebuilding my art career, which was challenging after ten years of being off track. I started painting again, dedicating an hour at a time to get back into the groove. Additionally, I earned my

Master of Liberal Studies and Art History in the winter of 2023. I've also become actively involved in various art associations and volunteer within local art communities.

At present, I teach art classes and create commissioned paintings. I join artists in exhibitions across America and abroad, and my artworks are collected internationally. Our home is in Burbank, California. Mic is 22, Angelina is 20, and JP is 18.

In 2018, I took my eldest son, Mic, to Vietnam. This journey allowed him to learn about my roots, the culture, and the history that has shaped my life. I dream of someday offering Angelina and JP the same experience and introducing them to this wonderful corner of the world.

Our family recently welcomed a new member, a darling, sweet puppy named Waffles, who continues to steal our hearts daily. Our beloved pet, Teepee, passed away in the summer of 2023 and will forever be in our family's memories.

Siblings- Oil painting by Mina Ho Ferrante

Micangelo (aka Mic)

My oldest son, Micangelo Ferrante, wrote this passage: "Wow, I'm in a book! My name is Mic - I'm the eldest son of my parents and two siblings. Thanks to my family and friends, I've had the best childhood a kid can ask for here in Burbank, California.

In kindergarten, I dreamed of becoming a Club Penguin video game developer. By first grade, I wanted to be an NFL Quarterback and fly to the moon. Now, at 22 years old, I have gained eighty pounds and recently graduated from the University of Southern California with a Bachelor of Music in Composition. I dream of being a film composer and the next Justin Beiber. Will my dreams fail? Only my chronic asthma will tell!

I owe everything to my parents, who have given me a life I cherish daily, and to Angelina and JP, who have stood by my side. They all inspire me on this journey, and I hope to share the love I've received with our future children and community, creating even more stories for the world to enjoy."

Angelina

Angelina's middle name, Anzi (written "An-Di" in Vietnamese), has a deep meaning. "An" signifies peace and is an ancient reference to Vietnam, as in An-Nam. Meanwhile, "Di," similar to chim di (a migrating bird), symbolizes flight in search of better conditions. Together, Anzi or "An-Di" translates to "a little bird seeking a peaceful home."

Angelina has been actively involved in the creation of this illustrative memoir. She wrote this: "I couldn't be more grateful for the opportunity to be part of writing my mom's memoir. Since I was young, she nurtured my creativity by encouraging me to explore painting, music, and writing. Those experiences shaped who I am and, as I grew older, led me to discover a deep love for storytelling.

This connection to such a strong and loving family history has become the foundation of my inspiration. It has driven me to pursue my dream of a filmmaking career, which I'm now working toward as a student at Loyola Marymount University's School of Film and Television.

My family's experiences in Vietnam created a multicultural environment that shaped our values of independence, empathy, gratitude, and community. My mom's worldview taught me to seize opportunities and appreciate life's blessings, which has profoundly influenced not only my artistic voice but also who I am as a person.

For that, I will always carry her lessons with me—in my art and how I live my life—and I hope those who read her book will be inspired to do the same."

Joseph-Paul (aka JP)

After graduating from high school, JP actively explores life's myriad possibilities. He has a passion for fashion and is the creative force behind his clothing brand, *Drexdworld*, which has a website at *https://www.deadtiredco.com/*. Lately, he's been enjoying the excitement of customers placing large orders for his clothing products online, a rewarding sign that his hard work and unique style are resonating with people. In addition

to his entrepreneurial pursuits, JP loves hip-hop dancing—and he's seriously good at it. He puts in a lot of time refining his skills, often training with dance teams and diving deep into the craft to keep leveling up.

MINA'S SIBLINGS

My oldest brother Elwood (aka "Bu")
Elwood wrote this following passage: Elwood currently works and lives in Silicon Valley with his wife, Mai Lien, and son, Jared. Mai Lien volunteers in the community with several charities while still working.

Jared graduated from San Jose State University with a degree in Computer Engineering. His hobbies include building custom keyboards and 3D printing. He is currently pursuing his Graduate Degree at Oregon State University.

Family portrait lithophane 3D printed by Jared Ho

Illustration by Zoe, Nu's daughter

My older sister Nu

Nu wrote this passage: "The post-pandemic economy has since forced the closure of Nu and Jack's restaurant, Aunt Mary's Cafe. While Jack decided it was time for him to retire, Nu is searching for her next endeavor. Their daughter Sông-An graduated from USC in 2022 with a BA in linguistics. However, during her last few semesters at USC, to overcome the challenges of Covid's online instructions, Sông-An took some photography courses and, since graduation, has shifted her focus to photography as a potential career."

Illustration by Xavi (aka Moka), Frank's youngest son, eleven years old

My younger brother Frank (aka "Bo") Kliment (aka Sữa), Frank's oldest Son, wrote this passage: "Frank and his family live in Santa Clara, at the heart of the Bay Area. His wife, An, takes pleasure in preserving cultural traditions within their household, all for the sake of their three sons: Kliment, Zidane, and Xavi. Kliment is passionate about learning new languages and aspires to earn a Bachelor's degree in Data Science at UCSD. A high school senior, Zidane dedicates his free time to pursuing his career as an up-and-coming video game developer. Meanwhile, the youngest, Xavi, follows in the creative footsteps of his older siblings. He enjoys exploring new clothing styles and gaining insights into different cultures. Frank and his family firmly believe that hard work will ultimately lead to fulfillment and success, as long as you are committed to seeing it through to the end."

My younger brother Yen (aka "Bom")

This is a transcription from Yen's interview by Angelina Ferrante: "We have four kids, ages 6 to 12, so life's definitely busy—but it's the good kind of busy. We stay active helping them with school, sports, and church activities. I work for the city—it's not super high-paying, but we make extra income renting out rooms in our backyard, which allows my wife, Nam-Trân, to stay home with the kids. Melody (Bon Bon) is in 7th grade, Socola (Francis) is in 4th, Takeo (Benedict) is in 3rd, and Coconut (John-Paul) is in kindergarten.

Weekends are packed: Saturdays are for church and youth group, Sundays are all about sports. We also love hiking, biking, hitting the beach, and trying new foods together.

Life isn't fancy, but it's full and meaningful. I look forward to retiring in 15 years, when the kids will be in college."

At the end of the epilogue, check out the comic strip "A Saturday at Hồ Gia"—drawn by Melody (aka "Bon Bon"), Yen's oldest.

Illustration by Melody

My youngest sister Phoenix (aka "Mi-Nhon")

Phoenix wrote this passage.

"Phoenix currently resides in Vietnam with her husband, Trang Nguyễn, and their son, Ian Ngo. She has been engaged in career development there since 2009. Her husband is an engineer, and their son is enrolled at the Saigon South International School.

Ian is an active member of his school community. He is a Varsity Volleyball team member and holds official positions in two school clubs. Growing up in an international setting, Ian has been able to befriend individuals from various nations, immerse himself in diverse cultures, and converse fluently in English and Vietnamese. As of the writing of this script, Ian is in Grade 12 and diligently preparing for his forthcoming university journey in the United States. Trang is transitioning from traditional engineering to the dynamic realm of Blockchain engineering. This transition is akin to 'building the plane while flying it', as he continuously learns new skills on the go and navigates uncharted territory to make things work. Despite the challenges, the family frequently visits California to reconnect with their relatives."

Illustration by Ian, Phoenix's son

The following comic pages depict a typical Saturday in Bom's family—most of the day is spent at church youth group activities and attending mass. They highlight just how much the kids enjoy being part of the Vietnamese Eucharistic Youth Society (Thiếu Nhi Thánh Thể). Artworks by Melody.

References

BBC News. (2019, January 9). Khmer Rouge and the Cambodian genocide before Vietnam brought troops to Vietnam. BBC News Tiếng Việt. https://www.bbc.com/vietnamese/world-46788950

Congressional Bills 111th Congress. (May 5, 2010). https://www.govinfo.gov/content/pkg/BILLS-111hres1331ih/html/BILLS-111hres1331ih.htm
the United Nations High Commissioner for Refugees estimates that over 250,000 boat people died at sea as a result of storms, illness, and starvation, as well as kidnappings and killings by pirates.

History.com Editors. (2022, December 12). Tet Offensive. History. https://www.history.com/topics/vietnam-war/tet-offensive

Hoang Huu Xung
https://nghiencuulichsu.com/2019/01/22/hoang-huu-xung-nha-su-hoc-dia-ly-viet-nam-the-ky-xix/

Ky Niem Ngay Xanh. (2018, July 10). https://www.facebook.com/media/set/?set=a.2039192149432537&type=3

Maria Mong Hoa. Catholic Pilgrimage Network. Retrieved January 5, 2020, from https://melavang.info/maria-mong-hoa/

Nguyen, Truong Thang. (2020, November, 9). Phi Hung Mot Hoa Si Tai Hoa Xu Hue. Antontruongthang's Blog. https://antontruongthang.wordpress.com/vh-ngh%E1%BB%87-thu%E1%BA%ADt/phi-hung-m%E1%BB%99t-h%E1%BB%8Da-si-tai-hoa-x%E1%BB%A9-hu%E1%BA%BF/

Phan, Hoang-Phu. Dai Nam Quoc Cuong Gioi Vung Bien. Ho Hoang Bich Khe. (http://www.hoangtocbichkhe.com/

Trần, Quan Chu. (n.d.). Tập sách Trung Tâm Thánh Mẫu Toàn Quốc La Vang, chương 4, phần 1. https://tonggiaophanhue.net/la-vang/gioi-thieu-la-vang/tap-sach-trung-tam-thanh-mau-toan-quoc-la-vang-chuong-4-phan-1/

Trần Quan Chu. Ơn Lạ Đức Mẹ La Vang, phần 3. https://lavanglasvegas.com/gioi-thieu/lich-su-la-vang-7/

Tran, Trung Sang. (2017, June 10). Nu hoa si dau tien dat da thanh. Quang Nam Online. https://baoquangnam.vn/van-hoa/nu-hoa-si-dau-tien-dat-da-thanh-50516.html

U.S. Department of State Archive. Hungary, 1956. https://2001-2009.state.gov/r/pa/ho/time/lw/107186.htm

Vua Thanh Thai (1879-1954). (n.d.) Nhan vat lich su. Retrieved January 5, 2020, from https://www.nhanvatlichsu.org/2019/11/vua-thanh-thai.html

Printed in Great Britain
by Amazon